tHIS tHEN

nANCY pHILBRICK-cUNNINGHAM

authorHOUSE®

AuthorHouse™
1663 Liberty Drive
Bloomington, IN 47403
www.authorhouse.com
Phone: 1-800-839-8640

My chatacters in Crossing Place seem real to me, for they belong beside
me here in Maine; yet, they and all about them are fiction.
1945 photo is printed by permission

First published by AuthorHouse   8/6/2010

ISBN: 978-1-4490-9923-7 (e)
ISBN: 978-1-4490-9922-0 (sc)

Library of Congress Control Number: 2010908167

Printed in the United States of America
Bloomington, Indiana

This book is printed on acid-free paper.

.BOOK. ONE.OF.tHIS.SERIES.

.tHIS. .tHEN.

.Finding.

.Common Threads. —

.in.

.Northern Maine.

.by.

.nANCY.

.pHILBRICK.

.eUNNINGHAM.

◇ tHIS tHEN ◇
Finding common threads in Northern Maine
... in a year of waiting for a soldier to return from Iraq

◇ nANCY pHILBRICK-cUNNINGHAM ◇

~

Thanks to my Soulmates: Susan Philbrick, Linda Hebert, Becky Wehel, May Philbrick, Leanne Philbrick, and Mags Philbrick.

~

Special credits to: Joan Philbrick Goodwin, Terry Philbrick Smith, Mike, Roxanne, Gina and her Four; Mary, Skip, Peter, and Paul; John, Norm, and our Fours.

~

Super credit to Ferne D. Kinsey, my neighbor over the fence, for suggesting that I write tHIS series and for pointing out things I needed to know!

~

Thanks, Ernie Kelly, the song writer!

~

Also, kudos to Shelia and The Green Jackets!

~

Dedication

To My Mother, Ethel May Larrabee Philbrick, who told me I was a
writer in the same way she reached out to people, invited them in,
kept in touch, found common threads to bring them together and
always had something interesting to say. In her Family Legacy, she
wrote **Thoughts to My Family** for her children, grandchildren and
Great grandchildren to come, telling them of her adventures and
her love for reading. As an author, I hold her words to my heart as
a challenge and inspiration when I write through my characters:
*"I had twelve children. I lost two little girls. I raised six daughters
and four sons. Of course, I think they are especially smart and
considerate. The best of it is they care about each other. That's what
I always wanted."* Because of Iraq, my mother waited again, as she
had sixty years before for her husband, her five brothers, and good
neighbors to return from WWII. She said having three children was
the miracle that got my father home, for the limit was two. Her
youngest son's daughter had three children under five and was still
sent to drive a tan truck in Iraq. Then came another miracle. Before
her Grandmother died, this soldier called to say she was coming
home. I care so much for that. We all do. Please note, my feelings
and awareness so tender, of this family I did not write.

◇And especially to Tigger, our four-footed common thread.◇

Dear Reader, in Crossing Place, the war *seems to be like wallpaper*, known but unshared until met face to face. And so, feelings on it between a young teacher and a young mother of twins may come sometimes together, sometimes apart, and sometimes cross paths, as common threads will do. Between Cinder and Frieda, it takes a bit.

This is to go on then >< ><   >< >< <u>This I have seen then</u>
Cinder Lorraine Smythe   Frieda Young
Country Chatoyant*   This For Two

What is   What is this for me,
this then   then?
here for me?

                                        Outside of where I am,
A line   an unknown harm
that is not mine   is wasting away a country.
What costs,   Life, dribbled and dibbled in the pocket.
to cro   Changed, forever.

An aura.   This I know then: "The unknown will be met
hopeful little thing.   in a better light when there is someone
Eclipsed by the bigger world of war.   with whom to filter it."

Being exactly it,   This I have seen then: "Sometimes we think
though.   people are as fragile
More to feel, give and hope for   as soap bubbles; until
in this space, in this time.   we see the rainbows inside of them."

Knowing this, then, I shall go on!   So, too, shall I.

> >< <> <> <> <> <> <> <> <> <> <> <> <> <> <> <> <>< <

*Chatoyant- /shaw.toy.awnt/ - chatty person, sometimes witty, always thoughtful.

Finding Common Threads that bring people together in tHIS tHEN

1. What's snow angels gots to do with it?

2. A new teacher and a Chatoyant (*shaw-toy-awnt*) in Crossing Place.

3. Sometimes we do wait a bit.

4. With or without foresight, familes grow and change together.

5. Off we go, now, to where more of the people in Crossing Place seem like heroes.

6. Details. Directions. Discussions. Decisions. Why Billy?

7 And what effect does a search on the mountain have on others?

8. 'Knowing what to do is part of a growth thing.' *Chatoyant*

9. Frieda puts it this way: "That is the way of life. When it comes, it comes right at you."

10. What happens, then, in February, gots to do with snow angels.

Dear Reader, You may use these Ten Threads to guide your reading. tHIS Author includes them where the ways and doings in Crossing Place can best tie into them. Two very special threads are not listed here. One is highlighted in your reading and is certainly powerful to those on the triangle and to others, as well. The other, which brings things together in the beginning, middle and end of tHIS tHEN, can come to you from your reading. Enjoy! *npc*

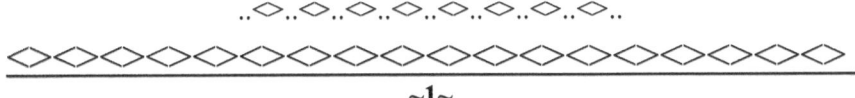

~1~

!What's snow angels gots to do with it?!

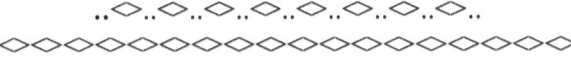

February get-away
in the Northern Maine Woods.
We are Outwitting old man winter.
Making snow angels.
Wanting to begin our life together.
But our President claimed first rights.
We have to wait.

vERN, *who is Ossie to Rachel*

Banking low for a landing upon the ice covered lake, Vern Paselli spotted them standing close together upon the shoreline. Snow had fallen in the night. It appeared light. Tree boughs showed only a whisper of white, but those crazy college kids were covered with it. Coming closer he saw why. They had made impressions in the snow all around where they stood. "Please. Think along with me. Think outside of the box. It's the perfect place to make snow angels," pleaded the petite red-headed girl, a college student by the name of Cinder Smythe, with serious green eyes and blushingly red cheeks. Made him reconsider his objections to flying her and her Rudd to this remote cabin in spite of warnings of a February storm that would leave him without a prayer of getting them out today if it had hit. Maybe they were just lucky. Maybe he could convince Rachel to come here and lay on her back beside him and make angels in the snow. Those crazy college kids. Making him think outside the box. He'd never thought of Rachel like that before. Not even his sister, Amy, knew what he thought about Rachel.

9

cINDER

"Who knows?" This Guardsman told this girl with half promise, half hope. "There may not be a war. Or maybe short like Desert Storm. Just in case, this then will serve to bind us, my dear, my little dreamer." Rudd put a delicately designed ring of strung beads and seeds, twisted together around colorfully coated fine copper wire upon Cinder's little finger. "Just so's you know," he told her. "I made it especially for you."

Cinder's strong response took shape within her ... as her words often did, for they were inspired from the Desiderata, *'Strive to be happy'* and *'Nurture strength of spirit'*. "Well," she cooed, "actually, there have been and will be much more then rings cometh forth to bind us together, my Soldier of Good Will To All Men ... and me."

Rudd laughed at her whimsical wit, as only he could laugh, abrupt and burstingly contagious.

At first, Vern Paselli, pilot and owner of the charter business, had staunchly refused to fly them to the hunting cabin because the weather report called for snow. "You could be snowed in up there. Maybe 'til the spring thaw." His eyes got very big, his brow, furrowed.

Cinder agreed. "Of course, it's a risk for you, too. But here's the thing. I plan to graduate college this year and Rudd's National Guard Unit plans to send him to Iraq for a year. You can't help us do that; but you can help us do this. My whole college campus is behind us. There'll be no other possibility. We can't chicken out."

Because the news had been featuring the President's talk about weapons of mass destruction and wanting to send troops to Iraq to blow them up, Cinder did not need to say that this might be the last time she and Rudd saw each other.

Paselli flew them, kept his cantankerous thoughts to himself.

In the spirit of their 'escape', Cinder did not waste their time together in sobbing away her remorse. She focused solely on Rudd. On why she loved him. His hugs, broad shouldered walk. His special ways to make her laugh. His forgiveness toward those who had wronged him in his young life. For Rudd was a strong man, firm and understanding toward others. She enjoyed the time they had. So, as she drew in the fresh morning scene around them, witnessed the remaining coals in the fireplace, the reddish glow against the caulked log walls, the ominous shadows across their piles of clothing on the old braided rug, she pressed her body against Rudd and stroked his shoulder, neck, and whiskered jaw. Wanted him. When light sharpened the shadows, she whispered seriously, "If this is what consummated means, I surrender."

His abrupt and burstingly contagious laugh burst out again as he drew her to where desire, warmth, and perfect joy were...consummated.

"I can almost taste the relish," sighed Cinder, dashing to fetch their clothing and bring them to their multi-quilted bed.

"Relish? You mean from when you were that gawky Freshman who caught my hotdog with your hair? I was so hungry, I could have eaten it, hair and all."

"You were one of those obnoxious Seniors who only come to Home Coming football games to ogle skinny cheerleaders." Under the covers, Cinder moved around Rudd as they struggled to sort their garments and get dressed.

"That's not fair. I came for the hotdogs!" Rudd fastened her bra.

"But you dropped it." Cinder helped him with his socks.

"Yeah. Then you dared me to have the first bite." Rudd pulled on Cinder's socks.

"Bite! Woof maybe. When you put it into your mouth all I had to bite was that little bit on the end. All covered with relish. On my side of your teeth." Cinder pulled him up to where she could look at him and ran her tongue around his lips.

"Whoa. You got the best part!" Rudd laughed again, his competitiveness showing.

"The kiss was the best part." Cinder turned a teasing face to him. "Our first. I confess, I knew it was coming." Pushing her lips to his, she added, "And I relished it!"

"Yes. That was the best. I got a keeper." His strong arms entwined around her. Then his hands cupped her cheeks as he tried to catch her tongue with his.

"I felt that way, too, Rudd, My Dearest Relish Breath."

"You mean, like I was a keeper?" Both, having had variable stability in their life, were glad to be a keeper.

"No," teased Cinder. "Hungry!" She let him win the tongue war. She had waited for Rudd in her Sophomore year, when he went to work for the United States Postal Service half a state away in Portland. Waited again in her Junior year, as he fought forest fires in the state of Washington and floods in Ohio with his National Guard unit. Now, in her Senior year, she would wait for him to come home from Iraq if the war came to be. Until they had first rights to each other again.

Alice and Mia, wives of their college Professors Ardean Paige and Fong Thi...all survivors of Vietnam, of the sixties...understood the feelings she and Rudd would be facing. Understood when Cinder told them, "His small apartment has paper thin walls."

"So what you need is a get away spot," surmised Alice.

"We had thought of a hunting lodge in the mountains for our honeymoon."

"A pre-nuptial honeymoon!" Exclaimed Mia.

"Pre-marital," laughed Alice. "And we can see to that!"

Alice and Mia organized 'A Soldier's Pre-nuptial Honeymoon Pop Corn Ball'. They sold bags of pre-popped corn, tins of corn to pop, corn dogs, and corn chips. For a dime, people could guess how many popped kernels were in one of the clear plastic snowballs and win the ball. They handed out free hot cider to those who came to skate 'n dance or take part in races. Each Participant got free popcorn. People were asked to light candles around an old milk pail that held cards and donations for the soon to be separated young couple. This then was to where Cinder and Rudd had come. Into the reality.

"Cinder Lorraine Smythe, promised wife, I'm going to miss you, girl. I'm going to miss the way you put thoughts to words and when you root for the Patriots and how you carry on about rivers that turn mountains into valleys." He kissed at her heart in the valley between her breasts. "I'm going to miss your burnt sugar pancakes." He lay his head there. Against her hard nipples. "I'm pleased to be a-honeymooning with you. I love you, Cinder. I'm sorry."

A gasp lifted Cinder to encircle Rudd in her arms and shoulders, to push her face into his hair. "I'm sorry, too, Rudd Wallace Vachon, promised husband. I wish we could seal our consummation in an envelope. Slip it into your backpack."

"Which part?"

"The part that rests against you."

"I meant, which part of our consummation."

"All of it. All or nothing. All of this and this and this. And even this." She tickled, kissed, hugged him. Laughing so she would not cry.

"Okay, for this then. You win. I'll save a spot."

All too soon they were outside with their backpacks. Trudging single file in the snow toward the lake. Happily together. No matter what was to come. Making snow angels as they waited for Paselli's plane.

tHE tHREE C's

While the country was still wondering why intelligence did not prevent terrorists from committing damage on 9/11 and why, with American troops still in Afghanistan, the President declared war on Iraq, pending orders were confirmed quickly. Rudd's last message to Cinder was to say he loved her and he was heading for Iraq inside of a week. He also sent her a form that gave her power of attorney over his affairs.

Students went routinely about their college studies; not being overly conversive about Iraq. To those who ventured an inquiry about Rudd's possible part in it or her supposed honeymoon, Cinder and her friends said Cinder was stunned and supremely grateful. The rest of her story was for Carla and Charissa.

Cinder, Carla and Charissa did not wear yellow ribbons or small lapel pins in the shape of flags to show support for the troops. Charissa called them an 'indulgent facade of patriotism'. "I come from the South," she boasted. "I don't know if the Civil War taught this country anything. It was food and bandages then and it's food and armor now!"

The Three C's met at the Bull's Den as they had every Saturday since they stood in line together to register for Freshmen classes. Vegetarians, they ordered cheeseburgers with lettuce and tomato slices on the side, a generous plate of home fries, and a supply of pickles and tartar sauce. An especially wicked sneak treat! It was a time to get down and personal. Today they sat in the corner facing the TV so they could watch the news reports on Iraq.

"Look! Enron! One sentence. California is sinking and it gets one sentence!" Carla poked her finger at the train of words that moved at the bottom of the screen.

"Sh! There's a real live soldier talking." Charissa leaned forward to study the background. "Just a Humvee and some sky. Do they always have blue skies in Iraq?"

"Well, they got sun," quipped Cinder, who also peered hard in order to see more than there was to see upon the screen. "Look! People are getting letters. There's one!"

An interviewed officer was saying morale of the troops was high and the soldiers were hoping to be home soon. There was a topography map behind him.

"He should know. He's got the map." Clara quipped. "Which one, hard to tell."

Cinder turned to her burger. "Well, my morale is not high. I don't have a letter from my weekend guardsman on assignment in Iraq."

"This assignment is orientated toward ridding the world of an evil dictator, Cinder. I don't think Our President thought of things like stamps," surmised Carla.

Charissa laughed. "I still don't get it. Terrorists knock down New York towers and while the world grieves, the news is filled with Saddam Hussein and weapons of mass destruction."

"I say this country began a collision course before the public syllabus was even written," sighed Cinder, attacking her hamburger.

"What would you call this then, Cinder? This course."

Carla was only probing her to get her to lighten up, but Cinder took the bait seriously. "I call it 'For Patriotism 0911'. A pass or fail. Hands on from the field, to the living room, to the newsroom." Cinder dragged a greasy piece of potato into a glob of tartar sauce on her plate, filling her mouth all at once.

Both Carla and Charissa rolled one hand in the air around the other. Rolled again, in reverse. A silent signal that Cinder spoke with mixed up thoughts.

"That way waiting families will be in the middle." Cinder repeated the signal and shook her index fingers at them. As she continued eating her fries, she explained what she concocted in a sexy voice. "Not at the end... not waiting for a report card...Progress Report. No longer torn to the quick. Be last to know. It's a personal thing you know, what's happening over there. Where's the Pony Express when you need them?" Cinder finished stolidly. Using humor to defray the void left in her life. Because of her selfish reality of it. Because of Rudd.

cINDER

Not long thereafter, Cinder's frustration over not hearing from Rudd seeped into dedicating her next piece for the Campus News to the soldier crisis in Iraq. Titled: *'The Catch of the Day'*. These were the daily TV media catch phrases that scrolled by in a word train at the bottom of the screen. She also questioned an embedded reporter's Humvee ride as to a foot soldier's eighty-five pound backpack and missing body armor. Cinder stated what she would not have written to Rudd: The media seemed to be into pushing the war rather than reporting it.

Professor Fong Thi rejected her article on its political impact. "This college should reflect an united American front. You can understand the realness behind that, Cinder. If you think it's a fantasy, then...."

"A fantasy? I can do that." Cinder's calm response was set upon by crashing sounds outside the granite blocked window of Thi's tower office. Thunder was now coming closer as each string of heat lightning cascaded across the massive sky outside.

Thi laughed. "If I know you, I think you just picked up a gauntlet. Maybe the gods are with you!" More crashing thunder came overhead as he added, "Humor or satire?"

Upon her feet at once, Cinder felt energized more by Thi's challenge than by the storm's electric sparks. "Both. But I'll need a special by line. And it will be a response column. Letcha know." She twirled her finger in the air and set off on her mission.

Thus Cinder's inner turmoil had a chance for a more relevant outlet. She wrote her weekly column by quoting and expounding upon comments she had overheard around campus and the community as a chatty person, possibly witty, fond of ponderous responses to human thoughts. She signed herself as: ***The Chatoyant (shaw.toy.awnt) ponderer of questions, comments, and remarks***.

Professor Thi asserted she had gone beyond humor and satire.

There began a good natured campaign around campus to unmask *The Chatoyant*. Thi's way around the snoopers was to take the responses home to pass them to Cinder through Mia, or Alice and Ardean Paige.

"Cinder, let this be a lesson to you," confided Mia.

"Oh?"

"Well, don't look at me to tell you. You're the one who's filling in the blanks to that question. By the looks at that mail piling up in these short weeks...well, you know you're onto something."

rACHEL

It was a beautiful Spring day. Having hung the sheets outside to dry, Rachel Aguila Romandez sat in the shade by the beautiful brook that came pure and sweet from the mountain. Perhaps Ossie would see and think of her if he flew overhead. An open book was on her lap. Today she was not reading. She was thinking of her family. How they had worked their way through six different states before earning their citizenship and finding real jobs in Maine. Of her sisters who had not come North with them. Luisa married a lawyer in At Lanta and ran her own hair salon. Anitia married an antique dealer in West Virginia and wrote Spanish verses for greeting cards and bookmarks for a publishing firm. Rachel's mother was happy for them. "I think this northern weather may have been too harsh for those tender beauties."

Rachel loved the big old house where she and her family lived together under one safe roof. At one time it had been a tourist stop. It needed a great deal of repair. Her two brothers, Juan and Vicente, were skilled carpenters. She helped them repair the roof, the stairway, floors, and walls. Mostly, she fetched and cleaned up after them. She helped her mother and father build furniture and picture frames. Together, she and her mother sewed colorful pillows, quilted vests, and bed and window covers for their family. All by hand and in the fine needlework her mother was shown to do by her mother.

After a time, Rachel's father took a counter job at Foley's Hardware, her mother baked backpack treats for Coughlin's Grocery and muffins for Murphy's Restaurant. Juan and Vicente, doing well now in their construction business, married their sweethearts, Marie and Elizabeth from Connecticut. Rachel and her mother made the wedding gowns for the double ceremony

Unlike her school friends, Rachel did not desire college or to get away from Crossing Place. She wanted to be near her family and be a waitress at Murphy's. So, for her High School graduation, her family bought her a sewing machine. Now Rachel made all the curtains, tablecloths, and napkins for Murphy's Restaurant. She designed a logo and hand stitched it to each piece. She also made a special Murphy line sold on consignment. Marie and Elizabeth worked at the Wal-Mart. They used Rachel's sewing machine to make doll clothing which they sold on the internet. Rachel used their patterns to make little Murphy Dolls.

It was left to Rachel to do the family laundry and cleaning. She liked that because she could always find time to go to the library for books. But that was not where she found her favorite book. Her bird book. Rachel had not spoken to anyone outside her family of the fear and terror they'd endured before good fortune came and helped them. She doubted that people who had grown up in such a sheltered, bountiful, quiet place as Maine would be interested in what had happened to her family. And yet she had confided everything easily and unabashedly to the big, gruff pilot when he walked her home and talked about birds.

The pilot came into the restaurant often. Rachel liked his manner. He tipped well, and she was pleased he chose her table. "How's The Pilot today?" She always asked.

"Hungry," he'd answer. "What's the special?"

Sometimes they talked about the weather. Sometimes they talked about the tourists. He always had a story to tell about a flying trip. It would be a few sentences here. A few more there. She always made a retort for him to laugh about while she attended other tables. Then on a day in early Spring, he remarked that the swallows had left Capistrano.

"What kind of swallow?"

He lifted his head from his coffee cup. "You a bird watcher?"

"Wait," said Rachel. She went around in back to her cubby to get her bird book. It was an old Peterson Guide a customer had left behind. "I've marked a few, see? I put the dates on them like the owner of this book had done."

He looked where she showed him.

"Is that good?"

"Yes. That's good, Rachel. Dating your sighting of birds."

"Do you sighting birds?"

"Well, you know what, Rachel? This here book you say was left by a customer? See here in the front? That name, there? Vern Oslin Paselli. That's me."

"That is you? I'm sorry. I did not know." Rachel shuddered and tried not to think what could have happened to her in Mexico if she had mistakenly taken a Gringo's book. In America, people were forgiven for tresspassings. They said so in Church. "I'm sorry. Please take back. I took good care of it."

He ignored her offer. "See here?" He opened the book to the section on swallows. "I've marked the ones I've seen. Let me show you my favorite sighting. October 6, 1988. I was 11 on that day and dreaming of being a pilot when I spotted an immature Osprey. Still in its nest. Crying for Momma. Most Ospreys had moved out by then. It was duck season. People shooting at ducks at the crack of sunrise. Ducks flying overhead. I watched that bird for days. Then one day it up and flew away with the ducks. Stayed right at their tail. What do you think of that?"

"I think that is a beautiful story. It is a beautiful bird."

"It's an Osprey. Os. Os. As in hossie. Pray as in Church. Os. Pray."

Rachel was very pleased at the exaggerated way he tried to pronounce the bird's name. All she could say was hossie, in her native tongue, with a silent h.

That was why she let him take her on a bird walk in spite of the threatening rain. Why she felt so comfortable around him. Why she liked him so much. Why she told him of the horror that had scarred her forever. Why she called him Ossie.

"I'm sorry." she sighed, hanging her head. "I don't know why I told you that."

He said, "I'm sorry, too. If I knew you better, I'd know if it were right to hug you after you've told me of your past troubles."

For all of her twenty-odd years, except for her father, Rachel had never been hugged by a man. "I'd like that," she said quietly.

"OK. Gotta make it quick, though. The birds have stopped singing and it's about to rain."

His hug, however, was very sweet and not hurried at all. After that, each time he came into Murphy's, the way he looked at her felt like a hug. Inside she felt herself singing like a bird. A timid bird. Afraid of flying. Afraid this pilot might not ask her to.

pROFESSOR tHI

Alice and Mia were convinced that their part in the honeymoon escape helped fuel Cinder's column. Thi was also certain of the column's value in these troubling times and was able to convince the administration of that. Yet he was astonished by the student response. Cinder's decision not to expose *The Chatoyant,* created a stir of excited interest followed by new volunteers to the Campus News staff and he was able to add a variety of new features. As did Cinder, he enjoyed the mystery. With the help of Mia and Alice, Cinder mischievously let on to others that she was learning to cook through editing recipes and researching food choices. She actually did try. Paige and Thi happily suffered the results. The women called it 'swallowing the evidence'.

In a short time, Thi saw his bi-weekly campus newsletter become a weekly event and its circulation double. More copies were requested from other campuses. Copies of his newsletter were included in college recruit mailings. Thi was assured of keeping his tenure. Because he had said no to Cinder Smythe, and because he was right to.

tHE tHREE C'S

Becoming focused on job interviews plus studying for their final exams, the Three C's looked forward to meeting at the Bull's Den to touch bases and see what's what. Clara and Clarissa had a job choice to report. Cinder had an unopened letter from Crossing Place.

"Why did you even take an interview there?" asked Charissa. "It can't possibly pay you what you're worth. As valedictorian, you could get one of the best contracts in New England." Charissa, herself, had opted to teach art in a private college in upstate New York for top bucks.

Cinder held the envelope to her heart. "Give me character. Give me a peaceful neighborhood. Where I can feel safe and wanted. I hold these things in great value."

"Oh, for God's sake, Cinder! Stop procrastinating and open it!" This from the new Assistant Director of Child Psychology Studies in Plastaid Research Hospital just outside of Boston, Massachusetts.

Cinder sighed, tauntingly giving in to Carla's prompt. She stood to give a clumsy curtsy...being as she was encumbered by her large leather cape and rain bonnet...to render it's impact. "I will be proud to accept a teaching position of Literature and Creative Writing to Crossing Place High School students near the territory of my honeymoon cabin."

"There's value in that, I have to admit. Pride, is it?" Carla raised her milkshake to make a toast. "To Cinder, who puts value in pride and money on the side."

"What about a place to live up there in the wilderness?"

"Well, Charissa, I've already withdrawn the balance in my college spending account. There's enough to get me a small apartment. Which, it says here, is ready for me, should I want it. I have enough to house me, feed me, and keep me happy until my first paycheck. To me, it will seem like a fortune! I might as well move in now. Now that I can't move in with Rudd."

It was official then, for the Three C's. New York, Massachusetts, and Maine would have the top three women students graduating from the University of Maine in Orono. The Three C's on a Triangle. Cinder's life was taking shape. Without Rudd.

cARLA

"PINK is not my favorite color, but it got me thinking," read Carla from her thesis. "That's it. The end."

"Whoa! You got me hooked. Now, I gotta think over how you laid this all out and came to a conclusion as to the use of color in perspicuous circumstances; but if I do, then I'm thinking and that's the point, isn't it? Even if I don't think the way you intended, it will be my thinking. So, I gotta tell ya, I'm thinking the color PINK is symbolic. Rights of women. Rights of voters. Rights in war. Make a difference. Go beyond. Not a time to speak softly and carry a plate of cookies. Sometimes you gotta yell! That's all folks!" Charissa blushed.

Carla was pleased with Charissa's summation of her work and clapped along with Cinder; but Cinder's reaction over Carla's long reading about war protestors who went abroad to join other protest marchers, surprised Carla.

"I remember a childhood chant-song about mud. Something about couldn't go around it, over it, under it. Had to go through it. That was humorous. Devious sales devises as propaganda isn't. The war in Iraq reminds me of that song. Fact is, it ain't fun to move through mud. PINK or not, fun or not, those ladies...up to their hearts. I enjoyed every gol dern word you wrote there about it. Got us to thinking, Carla. You're going to be a well received lady in that there psyche ward." Cinder tapped the paper with her napkin. "You know, you write like a Shirley Temple movie. Honest, not scripted."

"They give you five years. This is just the frosting. I'm going to interview some of those protestors. Find out what got them to publicly speak out. That's my point. What did they learn from doing it? How do they see the scenario now. If a picture is worth a thousand words, how many pictures does it take to make a good thesis?"

"Good point," said Cinder.

"I'm a fan of the everyday drama found in Folk Art and Norman Rockwell." Charissa said seriously.

"I've rather liked to hear a Jim Croce song." Cinder offered playfully.

"Me? I'm opting to get me a Mercedes Benz." Carla believed in the value of options.

When Carla scribbled the thoughts her friends gave her on the crib page, she felt encouraged. She could turn this pink idea into a quality piece of work. She just needed interviews and some news events. Maybe an end to a protested war.

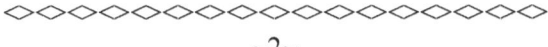

NeW TeAcHeR AnD a CHaTOYaNT

in CROssING PLACE!

cINDER

In May, two days after graduation and the day Cinder moved into her small apartment, the President stood on a ship and proclaimed the war was won. Or did he? Cinder listened to this speech again and again. His message was the same: He was not bringing the troops home. There was still more to do. Then she shuddered when he said, "Bring them on." Bring on to whom, she wanted to ask him. News channels showed American Soldiers toppling a statue outside of Baghdad as small numbers blipped across the bottom of the TV screen. Soldiers, without names or a specific reason. Dead. Why were they targeted? Did Rudd know them? Was he one of them? She wanted to know. She wanted to know why the President of the United States decided to parade around in costumes while soldiers were dying. Why reporters were embedded. Cinder felt the old helplessness, as if drowning, when she was taken from her Mother, lost her father. Rudd, too, had lived in several Foster Homes. And now he was sent to Iraq. Away from all he knew. Again.

What Cinder wanted was to keep busy. With Professor Thi's approval, she sent clips from her college writing to the Bangor Paper. She described herself as someone who had something to say on just about anything people wondered about in their lives. In truth, she hoped for another outlet for her inner thoughts. She gave her by line as *The Country Chatoyant (Shaw-toy-awnt)*. Her first offering set the tone.

This woman, a simple maiden missing her soldier, asked the Wall of Peace to help her. The Wall answered, 'Lo, it is not in my solidness to give this. Man has the road map. It is up to man to do what man has to do. And bring it me.' This woman jumped upon the wall. Walked upon it. She could not see to where she was going. Only to where she had been. A mist of her tears obscured even that. Climbing down from the wall, she sought direction from the Earth around her. She saw only space and time. Felt fear and loneliness. And anger from helplessness. This woman is not alone. I say to this woman and to each man, child and parent who await a soldier's return, 'Send armor, send food, and letters. One by one. Remember, the sun rises every day, birds molt feathers and migrate, tides come and wane, leaves change color before they fall, earthquakes shake and change the earth, floods overtake and subside, plants grow from seeds and self grown roots, but hair grows from childhood. There is more to be seen in this space, in this time. More to feel, to give, to hope for.

Her second, ran like this.

DESIGN A SOLDIER'S AMULET. Gather leaves, feathers, and grasses. Bind them together with tendrils of your hair; tie this into a bundle with your scarf or piece of clothing; or wrap this inside a pocket made of corn husks or newspaper. Tuck in items of supreme meaning to this conglomeration, such as a picture, a ribbon, a flower. Sprinkle in your favorite spices and incense. Thusly will you have made a special, personal and powerful amulet, more powerful than a proclamation, more binding than a promise, to send to your soldier. If you throw this Amulet as high into the wind as you can, the power of it will be carried across meadows, over rooftops, into rivers and

24

rising tides. Though the Wall of Peace is not for you as yet, that doesn't mean it will stay unchanged forever.I also say to this maiden, just as the sun's rays help clouds to form, just as clouds cover the sun, just as winds move the clouds, rains will stop falling and home your soldier will come to you once more. I, too, made an amulet for my soldier. For surely it will keep him awake on guard duty. When he returns from war, we will scatter his amulet before the Wall of Peace. And know that this man and this woman wanted it so.

Alysson Singleton, assistant editor for the Living Section of the Bangor paper, printed Cinder's piece, *The Soldier's Amulet*, because it seemed harmless enough. "It's not as though you could replace Dear Abby. It's more of a mythical agenda. Like a dream column. I'm only going on the success of your work in the campus press. Four columns."

Response was immediate. After her third submission, Alysson extended Cinder's contract indefinitely plus all rights in her name.

To get mail for her column, Cinder took the bus to Bangor once a week. People submitted drawings and photos and, oh, so many thoughts and questions! About life. Family. Friends. School. Travel. Even employment, war, and politics. Cinder responded to each entry. If not in her column, she sent one by post.

Cinder was not, as Clara warned against, a recluse. Firstly, she found her way around yard sales and flea markets, making acquaintances and finding what she needed to furnish her apartment. Secondly, the small library in Crossing Place had several high speed computers and offered free public access to the internet. Cinder needed only to put her disc into the slot and e-mail her work to the Bangor paper. Thirdly, she found a place to volunteer. In that marvelously charming library.

"We could use help anytime," Blayne Roderique, Head Librarian, confided in her quiet, confidential tone. "Most of our volunteers are older women, quite set in their ways. If you could just fill in where you see a need without overstepping, you know? Where one might think you were in charge? That would be great." She added cautiously, "I sound like an anxious old maid, don't I?"

"Oh, are you?" laughed Cinder.

"Not on the shelf yet," replied Blayne. "And I should know!"

Cinder was always busy in this tiny, town library with its interesting pace of doing things. She e-mailed Charissa and Clara this way:

> June. I wear socks to bed. Sweaters on walks. Mornings have fog. The Dampness lingers well into morning. May as well be in Ireland! Green, always on the mountains. Well worn paths to get just about anywhere and see a view. I love it here. Blackflies and all! People are friendly, but close to themselves. Like there's time to get acquainted and they don't mind taking it. Content with tourists; but I'm a come lately. An Outlander! I volunteer at the library. People wave to me when they see me at the store, or walking. You know, slowly taking ownership of my presence. So, lately, they comment on my socks.   Cinder of the Three C's

Missing Rudd, Cinder wished she could jump that benign Wall of Peace to fetch him home! She missed his hugs. His jokes. She wanted him back in her life, hear his abrupt and burstingly contagious laugh again. Cinder arranged her writing area by her North window, where the light was best, to keep an eye out for their honeymoon plane. Watch for changes on the mountain. Watch her mailbox. She did not wait in vain. However, when it came, she carried it to her apartment and sat quietly before her writing window before she tore it open!

RUDD's Letter to Cinder

> Dear Cinder,
>
> It's not a good place for a Honeymoon, but some of us are having fun down here. My face is getting black from the sun. God. I can't tell you how much fun it is to get clean. Sometimes it's the only

fun. There's this guy. His name is Smythe, like yours. I checked him out first thing. He says he's sure you must be related 'cause he's true black. True being the key word. This guy is an honest to God human being. Cracks us up with his jokes. Yeah, we got a few gals around here, too. Four tents away. I hear them giggling sometimes. If we stayed together long enough, we might get like those guys in M.A.S.H. We don't hear tell of much, other than what is right here in front of us. We eat, go out, and sleep together. We're never alone.　　　　　I told Smythe about our snow angels. He made me get right down on this sandy soil and show him what I was talking about. Then he got down and swooped his hands and feet around like he was really in the cooling snow. Then the other guys were doing it. Now we got something to talk about when it gets too hot to breathe.

Sounds like you've been busy as ever. And clever. Thanks for sending your picture. And I liked that story you wrote about the Wall. When you gonna send me an amulet for real, my little dreamer? All smelly and such. I might not get all your letters. Just keep sending them once a week and I'll do the same. Send that plane down here anytime! <u>This is Rudd, who loves Cinder</u>

cINDER

　　　Since Rudd's letter, it was a small reach for Cinder to begin some of her columns with thoughts of woman hunting man, catching man, and sending him into manhood. As she wanted for Rudd. True to his asking, she wrote him once a week; yet there were no more letters from him. Over laundry in her apartment building's basement, she confessed her concerns about Iraq to Emily Simone. Emily was a registered nurse and lived in a large apartment just above Cinder's little one.

　　　"There's another world out there," Emily told her. "It's called talk radio. Not the vulgar stuff the likes of that High Noon Anti-sensitivity! Did I say that? I'm just a Clear Channel fall out. In the afternoons, I get a great feed off the internet. All the way from Florida. She's on for hours.

She makes me feel like laughing and is ever so rounded when it comes to knowing what the rest of the world knows. Come by for coffee sometime. Listen in. Tuesday at three o'clock. I get off work early. Bring some of those muffins I smell you cooking. And something to do while you listen."

Cinder did just that. What she heard made her cry. Not so much because what she heard was not what she had thought, but because she actually heard someone in the media saying it. Not yelling and referring to something sexual. It was because there had been so many yells and so many things not allowed to be said and so many times she had wanted to hear someone demand an answer to a question and follow that thought through, she was filled with relief. "I didn't know, Emily, that guessing about the this's and then's had been so hard on me. Why, it's some kind of eye opener to hear what the rest of the world is hearing. I didn't know that Clear Channel had so much control."

"It's OK. Look, when you come next time, let's work together on a quilt. I've always wanted to make one for charity. Maybe you can find a book with patterns at the library. I got lots of cloth scraps. I've got scissors and a sewing machine. Needles and thread. I just don't know where to start. How about it?"

Cinder told Blayne Roderique about her visit with Emily. Blayne belonged to a quilting group. She gave Cinder cardboard pattern pieces for a simple, colorful lap quilt and a supply of cotton batting. "And," said Blayne with her eyes twinkling, "Once you finish that quilt, I know just the place for you to donate it. Of course it will be hard to know which of the dozen or so Meals on Wheels people should have it."

Emily was just as excited to hear of this as Cinder was. And so, because of Rhandi Rhoades, they would surely have a dozen lap quilts completed before Cinder's school year started.

aMY

Often her brother, Vern, joined Amy; yet she preferred to be alone. These were the hardest and most buoyant moments for her. When the heat of August came. When she and her crew worked feverishly to fill the large orders for her greenhouse customers. When she made her daily visits to her father's grave and laid fresh flowers there. And upon the smaller one at his side for her mother who died when Vern was born. *"Loss is a personal thing,"* their father had said. *"You can put love and hope into it if you want. It's easier than trying to let go of it. It's like planting seeds."* He always said things like that. He believed she and Vern would grow just fine. *"Growing is what's important."*

Amy looked forward to September rains. To fewer customers and larger orders. Roses, bulbs, floral arrangements, house plants. She expected the bulb rush to be as profitable as any year; however, she was also expecting this to be a good year for holly, mistletoe, and poinsettias. She was already doing a great business in wreaths, for the forest was bountiful with offerings for the makings. No doubt, the winter here in Northern Maine would be a cold one. This morning she left her motley crew furiously working in the potting and growing sheds under Frieda's watchful eye while she went over to Murphy's for coffee and bagel.

When Rachel stopped by Amy's table with more coffee, she put the coffee pot on the table and opened Amy's Bangor Paper to a column that was dedicated to Words of Woman and Man. "Have you read that new column, Amy? *The Chatoyant*? **Others have gone before you, Woman said to Man. But none have walked in your shoes as you must do.** Is this from an Indian saying?"

Amy was most interested and said, "Everyone needs to take steps, Rachel. With or without shoes, or tried and true paths."

"You mean like someone went this way and you want to go this way?" Rachel demonstrated her words by taking small steps and then big ones. Then she walked around a table, did an about face, and retraced her path by going backwards.

"Walk this way. Walk this way," the people at another table chanted. They, too, had read the column. And these were men.

Although Amy knew that Rachel knew the intent of those words was far more serious, Rachel had an encouraging way to demonstrate the differences in the ways of people. No one at Murphy's that morning would forget that. Amy decided to save this piece for Frieda. Or anyone else who had a difficult row ahead of them. She posted it near the cash register of her shop. As she did for the next column and the next.

cINDER

Emily joined Cinder in taking some of the children from the apartment building to the park or to baseball games. There were many people there that knew Cinder from the library. Emily said that before she met Cinder, she never got to meet so many people, and she was a native. A few times, Cinder shared one of Rudd's letters. Emily often shared one from her cousin. Cinder turned to Emily for support when a letter came from Rudd to say he had been wounded.

"Rudd says he was hospitalized in Georgia for a month. What he did not say about that scares me. I am glad and fearful and proud of him. He writes. 'I am better now and am being shipped back to Iraq where my unit is on guard duty outside Baghdad. On August tenth. I could not get permission for you to visit or to visit you. They said it was for security reasons. They lost my request card or something. That's the bad news. The good news is, I'll be stationed in one place and will be able to e-mail you when I get back to Iraq. I'll go through old Ardean Paige so he can connect us. I could use a fill up for that spot. What you got?' "

"Rather short piece," mused Emily. "Sounds quite sure of himself. I could love a guy like that."

"Well, I do," stated Cinder with a passion. "And I'm glad he didn't call. I may have faltered under the separation sentence his untouchable superiors put between us. I'll just hold my head high and tell myself that what is done is done. All I can do is try to firm up Rudd's sense of will. She told Emily, "If it's a fill up he wants. It's a fill up he gets."

Her Rudd would be needing a more powerful amulet. Stronger than day old bread! She wrote, "Cinder faithfully loves Rudd," and filled the envelope for him with ashes of incense, a slip of her hair tied in a bow, and a picture he had taken of her when they were on their pre marital honeymoon. On the back she had written, "The rest of this story is relished." She wrote to

Rudd everyday now. She sent Rudd clips of her newspaper column. Rudd's letter had come in August. Professor Paige had no messages from Rudd, but encouraged her on her column. He and Thi encouraged her to read the Bangor Paper.

By now, Cinder had another outlet for her mind to go. Set up her classroom and attend the mandated teacher workshops. One meeting discussed an outline guide for discussing the war in Iraq with their students.

"Is this about French Fries?" One teacher at Cinder's table remarked good naturedly. Some people laughed over the idea that because France had voted against UN support of the war in Iraq, there was a boycott suggested on French Fries and the Statue of Liberty. Most of her new colleagues seemed reticent, so Cinder stood to comment. "First, let me say, I know the difference between French Fries and Home Fries. It's McDonald's, Right? I also want to remind you about crabs and lobsters. Just because crabs and lobsters have a crust that turns red when boiled. A crab may be more of a pink. It's not true that they walk the same. Right?" Cinder looked around at the blank faces turned toward her. "You know, crabs walk sideways." There was a smattering of laughter, then, followed by applause. "Well, my point... although I am taking a bit long to get to it...mainly because it is getting close to lunch and I am craving some good old hash browns and blueberry cobbler...my point is I expect a lot from my students. I expect them to be honest and able to make the courageous decisions they will be called upon to make because of this war. Especially after. I personally realize that our young people may be required to take ... to stand up ... and cover the fallout when our President says 'Bring it on'. The only thing about this war we know for sure is that tax breaks are not geared to pay for it. I see that as a problem. I do not wish to propagate the media agenda ... i.e. lack of credibility. Or take issue in my classroom against this war ... which I am not ... or for it ... which I am not. I shall choose my words carefully, but I will not lie, indulge, or distort facts. I shall encourage, not discourage, my students to think outside of the box. How else are they to be resourceful enough to be all that they can be? No pun intended." It was not a reach for Cinder to say these words. She felt them to the quick.

"Wow," said a teacher to her right. "I wish I had said that." He stood up to say, "I was thinking along those same lines. It's clear to me that students are the people we once were. Can't say as I'd have liked to have a teacher restrict my sources of knowledge. Well, they were restricted in some cases. You know, by busy work."

Teachers across the room cheered, "Yeah, Kevin!"

"I think the internet restricts me from knowing as much as students today because they have more time than I do to use it." So offered a distinguished looking lady teacher from across the room.

"So they tell us," chided a rather plump teacher beside Cinder. His tag read Len Harris.

"I think we would come out on the short end of things if we stuck to this outline exactly," continued Kevin Young. "We can accept this outline as a guideline with the emphasis added that we will assist our students to be all that they can be. Right?"

When he sat amidst guffaws and a smattering of applause, Cinder whispered, "Thanks. You've restored my faith that teachers are good people, able to think and lead, not just follow an ambiguous agenda."

He responded with, "I like to think outside the box. But I'm mostly doing history."

As far as the outline went, Cinder's new working partners accepted it as a work in progress. To be continued and updated in future meetings. Kevin Young volunteered to track notes on comments and pitfalls.

To Cinder, their meetings were more lively after that. In her mind's eye, she could hear Mia say she was onto something. She took this experience into her weekly column.

> *The strongness in people faith is that there is no shaking of it from the tree of consciousness, no hiding of it from tents to castles, and always a warmness of it in the hearts of those who seek it, give it, or are inspired by it. As children often are.*

..><.><..◇◇◇..><..><..◇◇◇..><.><..

~3~

¦S.o.m.e.t.i.m.e.s w.e D.O w.a.i.t. a b.i.t.¦

◇◇◇◇◇◇◇◇◇◇◇◇◇◇◇◇◇◇◇◇◇

fRIEDA

Kevin, sleeping soundly, Frieda Young closed the windows against the rain. As she often did in quiet times, she filled her thoughts with poetry for their twins, Kade and Dean.

> *Rain drops*
> *eat dust*
> *from window panes.*
> *That's why*
> *we have to wait a bit.*
> *Before washing*
> *the uneaten parts.*

There was a time when they'd bump in the dark. Trying to close the same window. That stopped after the twins were born. That's when she became the care giver. The keeper of windows in the dark of night. Of garbage on Thursday's. Of doctor appointments and hair cuts. Of collecting and redeeming soda bottles. Of cooking perfect meals and waiting for Kevin to join them. Of not minding if he had already eaten because her leftovers mostly got gobbled later. He the teacher. So busy. Never told his sons about raindrops.

"Couldn't sleep?"

"I got up to close the windows."

"Why? It's hot in here."

"Better than being wet also."

"Better than also being wet. Raining? Rats. I have a fieldtrip today."

"It's three AM. Can't your fieldtrip wait?"

"Very funny. You should write a poem about it. Tell the boys."

"I can wait until I wake up."

Maybe when she awoke, the lumps in her breast would be gone and the university had not moved the publication date of her poetry book from February to June. The good side of that meant she could have her secret surprise served up with strawberries, cake and ice cream at a celebration party in the summer. When her husband's head wasn't preparing for a new school year. The sad side was that inside of those nine months she could be dead. She lay quietly on her back until even breathing convinced her Kevin was asleep. Then she wiped the tears from her nose and ears and made up poetry in her head until thunder pushed her into sleep.

> *Up went the sun.*
> *Out came the clouds.*
> *Along came the wind.*
> *Came also the chirping birds.*
> *You'd have to be there to feel it.*
> *The hotness.*
> *The stilling of the breeze.*
> *Rain spilling down all at once.*
> *Silvery drops causing shivers on bare arms.*
> *Rain showers create fun places to run free.*
> *Until the lightning strikes the thunder.*

"Kevin?" He was up already, had not stirred her. She lifted the quilt to find her slippers, pulled on her old cotton robe before treading down the stairs. The twins were eating cereal and toast with TV.

"Which one of you guys gave you permission to be so quiet?"

"It was a tie, Momma," they said in one voice. As if she didn't know.

Kevin was already at the door. "There's a phone message for you. Gotta go. I made fresh coffee. Took some bills from your purse. Have a nice day." All that remained of Kevin were his breakfast dishes stacked on the counter. Frieda fetched his half filled coffee cup and stuck it into the microwave. She listened to the phone message.

"Good morning. This message is for Frieda from Doctor Eiser's office. When you come in for your appointment this afternoon, don't forget your urine sample. We look forward to seeing you at 1 o'clock."

"What's urine?" asked Kade.

"What's sample?" asked Dean.

"Urine is pee. A sample is just a bit of it. I wasn't planning on taking the whole toilet to the doctor's office," Frieda grasped her hands together away from her stomach to demonstrate carrying a toilet bowl.

"You're funny, Momma!"

Frieda hugged her laughing boys. "I'm going to let you stay with Grandmumma while I visit Doctor Eiser."

"You mean Kade or Dean?" Asked Dean.

"You mean Dean or Kade?" Asked Kade.

"I mean Kade and Dean. I mean Dean and Kade. First I'll take you to Daycare and then I will pick you up and take you to Grandmumma's."

When they got to Daycare, Dean whispered in one ear, "I hope you have time to urine, Momma." Kade whispered in the other, "I hope you have time to sample, Momma." Her sons squealed happily as she chased them to the door.

Mondays were always hectic at the plant nursery. Frieda did not mind. It was the kind of day she needed to keep her from worrying. Pack this. Pull this. Throw this. Answer this. Find this. Order this. Fill this. Clean this. Smile all the while.

"Not a good day for you to leave early," complained Amy.

"Never is," answered Frieda.

"Don't let that stop you."

"I won't," responded Frieda.

"Don't bother coming back."

"I won't," repeated Frieda.

"And don't come in tomorrow if you feel sick."

"I won't," she agreed. Her boss hugged her, patted her shoulder.

Amy Shirly was as tough a business woman as they come. Also tough on keeping her workers happy. "It's our business to make people happy," she'd remind anyone who had a problem with her being nosy toward their private life. "You can depend on that." Frieda did. Amy was the only one who knew about her lumps. After today's doctor's appointment, Frieda planned to meet Amy at Murphy's to discuss what was to be done about them. Frieda thanked Amy with these words:

> *The unknown*
> *will be met in a better light*
> *when there is someone with whom to filter it.*

A bicycle accident caused an emergency. The young mother was quite distraught. The child wailed upon her lap. The mother cried louder.

"For Heaven's sake," corrected Frieda. "You can fall apart later. Right now you should be strong for your child. Stop babbling. And tie your shoe."

Both child and mother were stunned by Frieda's interference. Long enough for the nurse to extract the injured child from his mother's grasp and carry him into the examining room. The mother stopped to tie her shoe. Frieda, mother of twins whose father was prone to fall apart in emergencies, wished she'd had the courage to talk to Kevin like that. She silently opened a Family Circle magazine.

Amy was waiting for her. "Two cups of coffee and a bagel late you are," she pronounced with a wave to Rachel to please bring more.

"This Mom had a kid with a broken arm. I would have traded places if I could."

"When do you plan to talk to your Mom?" On a full stomach, Amy was direct.

"I don't know."

"Frieda. This is not just happening to you, you know. You've got to let someone in your family in on what has got to be the most traumatic thing in your life since puberty. If not your Mom, then Kevin?"

"The ... the ... the autopsy came up malignant. So the strategy is to whack off my breasts. Both. I don't know how to tell Kevin that."

Amy shook her head. "That's biopsy. So are you gonna wait and walk in one day and say, 'Hey, Honey, you know those breasts you haven't been fondling lately? I had them removed. See. Whaddaya think?' " Amy gestured as though opening her blouse.

"God, that's dramatic!"

"Not very realistic. What next?"

"Blood tests. Another scan. Strict diet. No coffee. No sweets. No toast or eggs. No Milk. Operation. The usual."

"OK. So let's splurge before you purge. How 'bout we have strawberry shortcake with chocolate sauce and extra Coolwhip?"

"Amy! You just ate two bagels! How can you?"

"Because I've been where you are now. One, anyway. Can you guess which?"

Amy had not reached across the table, but Frieda felt as if she had! "You are remarkable. I'd never have guessed. Let's celebrate!"

During the splurging, the girl talk turned to serious issues. Insurance. Child care. Sex and marriage vows. Faithfulness. Kimo therapy. Hope. Falsies. Implants. Vacations.

"I pray to God you don't hurt as much as I do." Amy held onto her stomach.

"I think I do and I feel so bad for you!" Gushed Frieda.

The women laughed and cried and hugged each other.

"See you tomorrow," Amy flipped over her shoulder as she unlocked her car door. "Forget what I said about not coming in. I want to see how you survived that shortcake."

Frieda watched as her Mom, Victoria Abbot Harrington Coumbs, packed the twins into the car. A woman who had survived two husbands. How cruel it would be to lose a daughter, too. "Dean and Kade said you had to take an urine sample to the doctor's. Didn't you take one last week? I've never heard of two in a row unless something is wrong. Is there?"

Frieda hugged her Mom especially well. She noticed she had great color for a woman her age. "There is, Mom. Doctor Eiser wants to do more tests. Blood and pictures. I already got a mammogram."

"You mean x-rays?"

"You know, that thing they do with jelly and rubbing a sound thing over you."

"Sounds serious. Let me know if you want me to come with you, Frieda."

"I will, Mom." It was a beginning. She could try again later.

She could talk to Kevin also. She could also try to talk to Kevin.

kEVIN

Kevin could not wake her. Didn't want to wake her. He heard the way she shuffled around, stepping carefully in the dark and closing windows. He hoped to god she wasn't pregnant again. Then he hated himself for thinking that. They hadn't had sex for months. Something wasn't right. Watching her breasts heave in the morning light, stirred him some, but not enough. He tried to remember what it had been like between them before the twins were born. Before their life became shaped into routines. He wanted spontaneity again. He wanted to feel the excitement of full, lush lips sending shocks into his loins. Arms that held and held. Not letting go when a kid sneezed or cried in the night. He wondered if other men felt this way. If he'd find the same thing with other women. Another woman.

Sitting in his favorite spot in the teacher's lounge, Kevin watched Cinder Smythe burst through the door and become the center of attention. Certainly his. Ever since he'd gotten to his feet to back up her little speech about crabs and lobsters. How vibrant she was. So young and innocent. Always with a word for everybody. Not like Frieda had been at her age. Not now. He wondered what it would be like to bed her. To be made to feel like a king again. The way Frieda once made him feel.

"Hey, corner person, want a muffin? It's apple and cinnammummmum."

She made him laugh. He did not correct her as he did Frieda.

"If you like it, there's a recipe on the table. Do you?"

Kevin took a bite and said he did. He took the recipe for Frieda.

After his first class, Kevin met his study group in the cafeteria. The announcement came over the intercom that their bus had arrived and they could board anytime. There was a flurry of excitement when some students came in to say that Len Harris, his team teacher, had sprained his ankle on the front stairs and was being helped to the nurse's office; and other students came in to tell Kevin they had convinced Miss Smythe to cover for Mr. Harris so they could go on their fieldtrip.

Kevin's breath stuck in his chest when he saw Cinder struggling into a woolen jacket embroidered with a remarkable eagle across the back. Her long red hair seemed to be tickling it into flight.

"I hope someone will share a lunch," quipped Cinder. "Where are we going anyway? Does it have to be a surprise?"

"We're working on genealogy, Miss Smythe. Where do you think we're going?" She guessed it was Josh Fortier who spoke.

"You don't mean," said Cinder. "You're ghouls from school?"

"Just stick with us, Smythe," Offered Dannel Harris, with a wide grin. "We won't let those stones hurt you!"

"Okay. Take charge of your weapons, troops. Let's board the bus." All students willingly followed as Cinder waved her hand in the air.

Kevin had the presence of mind to take attendance. Rain or shine, this would be a fun fieldtrip. Cinder would see to that. The bus trip was jovial and talkative; no thrown pencils, stolen notebooks, or grabbing hats and snacks. Cinder demanded quiet once they passed the entrance to the graveyard by a wave of her hand. Kevin could not have done it. The rules to this adventure were now in the hands of the mighty adventuress. Kevin didn't let himself think that he was taken in under her spell as these teenagers were. He let it be. Enjoyed feeling relaxed amongst them. And stared at Cinder.

Groups dispersed respectively toward designated lots. Then returned to the bus to share what they had found before the sprinkling rain turned to a down pour.

Kevin snapped two rolls of film with his Polaroid for an immediate record of what they saw. Cinder, in some of them. His hand made it, too. With his ring finger. Proof he was the only married person on the trip. Even the bus driver was single. He did not let that make him feel old or uninteresting. He let it make him feel he had a meaning in life.

There was no dampening in Cinder's spirits. She seemed to bounce upon her seat in the front of the bus even when it wasn't moving. And eat! Three sandwiches to his one. Students fell over themselves to share with her, joke with her, and listen to her. This is the way fieldtrips should be, thought Kevin. He surveyed the group with a fatherly air. Answering their questions and giving suggestions. The library research went quite well. Here Cinder deflected ominous glitches toward Kevin. He liked being the go to guy. He carried that feeling home with him. He hoped his evening with Frieda would go as well. The glitch was, there was no Frieda. And no note to tell him when to expect her home. Then he wondered if the boys were still in Day Care. Had Frieda worked late? Had she left a message for him at school? He called the number.

"No. Dean and Kade are with their Grandmumma. I think Frieda had a Doctor's appointment. I'm pleased you checked. Kids like that."

He should have remembered about Doctor Eiser. He should have talked to her about it. About picking up the twins. He popped a beer. He might as well cook a burger and bean casserole. She always liked the way he cooked it. While it simmered, he stirred up some raspberry jello for the twins. They liked to slurp it from their spoons. He did too.

By the time his family came home, Kevin was on his third beer. He had mellowed from the high he had felt during the fieldtrip. His expectations toward Frieda had dimmed to being respectfully civil. He apologized for not helping with the boys. He helped now. Helped them hang their things and wash up for supper. Frieda mentioned the emergency at her doctor's office as to why she was so late. He thought she was holding something back; but because he fell asleep on the couch before she returned from putting the boys to bed, he didn't ask. When he finally stirred enough to get himself to bed, Frieda was asleep.

Had Kevin not been drunk and not thinking in awe of Cinder, the way his wife lay in bed may have filled him with manhood. Instead, seeing her upon her back with her arms crossed below her breasts and her hands cupping them, he felt rejected. He wanted to puke up the bean casserole all over her. The thought made him laugh.

Frieda stirred toward him. "Was it a good fieldtrip, Hon?"

"Sure. The rain cooperated. Got some nice pictures to show you."

"Me, too. I got them today."

"No kidding. I thought you went to see the doctor."

"I'm so sorry, Kevin. I didn't get good pictures. Can you hold me?"

Kevin hesitated. "Sure. Be a minute." He took ten. Cleaned up after himself in the bathroom. Shucked his clothes and crawled in bed beside her. She did not respond to the weight of his arm around her. Still he kept it there for sometime in case she did. Not that he'd do anything. He needed to sleep. An In-service Day. He wanted to be clear headed.

fRIEDA

Seeing Kevin with a beer on a weekday disturbed Frieda. She turned to her notebook and wrote about it there ... in private.

> *When are people like elephants?*
> *When they drink beer, dear.*
> *When are people like raging elephants?*
> *When they drink too much beer, dear.*

What she had to tell him would definitely have to wait. Still, he had fixed a fine supper for them. She had to hand it to Kevin. How he could come through sometimes. She thought his fieldtrip must have gone awry if he was drinking. She would eat his prepared meal if it killed her. By the time she made it to bed, she thought it had. That and the strawberry shortcake. She crossed her arms to hold her stomach in place. Her hands patted her breasts to feel their softness. The softness that would become scar tissue. Kevin's laughter prompted her to tell him about the mastectomy; but when she heard him expel his supper in the bathroom, she knew it was not going to happen. Rather than reach out again, she let herself fall asleep.

cINDER

The sprained ankle thing gave Cinder an opportunity to see her new school at its best. In spite of Len Harris's pain and being smothered by attention, he expressed surprise and genuine pleasure when he learned she would cover for him. He couldn't thank her enough. Then there was Kevin Young. Kevin seemed ingratiatingly grateful. He didn't stop ogling her during the whole fieldtrip. Like she was a goddess! Neither of these men, irregardless of the state she found them in, could hold a candle to her Rudd; but they could give her lots to write about. People were like unread books... hard to judge by their covers. For now, she had a more personal topic. Students promising to protect her from the monoliths in the graveyard!

> *Raindrops fell today as I walked around stones of many shapes and sizes. Each one marked a past I had not known. I was not afraid of them. Nor unsure of what I was to do. In fact there was laughter from those who were there with me. We searched together. Communicated and learned from each other. And I felt safe. Neither wet nor tired. Yet hungry for bread. Craving food for my thoughts and musings. Either man or matron would be pleased to behold such caring in a graveyard.*

That Rudd would be home soon to read the responses to her column was an old thought now. Since Labor Day, reports revealed that soldiers were doomed to stay even longer; and soldiers were being shot, dying from roadside bombs everyday. Hopes did not look good.

Most all the adults working at Crossing Place High School were married. Husbands and wives. She and Racine Elliot, both in their first year of teaching, were single. Racine had a fetching story to tell about that. "You see, in our grade school, we had all female teachers. And they all got pregnant within a year of their first day there. The rumor said there must be something in the water. The girls in my fourth grade class stopped drinking the water as soon as they knew. Like, water impregnated girls who hadn't reached puberty!"

"For sure. I'd have believed it. At that age."

Racine blushed. "Well, I'm one of the gullible ones. Take my word. I'm not going to research on how long people work here before getting married. That got swept off my slate months ago. After a year here, I plan to head South. I mean to find a position below the Mason Dixon Line. Then I'm going West. Probably find someone out West. Settle down. Raise some gullible fourth graders."

Cinder, since her speech at the workshop, wore a button with a picture of Rudd in his National Guard uniform to show that the president's war had a personal twist for her. Her fellow workers showed concern for the troops. For Reservists and National Guardsmen being sent to Iraq. Whether weapons of mass destruction were there, or not. Most wore yellow ribbons to show their support. In her column, Cinder wrote about what did not show.

"We know and love them as men and women, girls and boys, these soldiers who are now far away. They will not be home for supper. We can still keep the light on for them. Keep them close by in our thoughts. In the window of my mind's eye, I picture my soldier waving at me from the small plane that flies over the mountains. I wave and throw a kiss. Pretend that one day, when I least expect it, the pilot will be him. I know he will come home to deliver the mail once more. Wishing he were here, I yearn to hear the words he whispers to his amulet."

If a copy of this column reached Rudd, he also got a copy of a more personal version.

By ten o'clock, Cinder pulled the last tray of popovers from the oven. With lemon and apple filling they were sure to be a hit at the coffee table for her high school's In-service day workshop. She planned to gather a smattering of comments over them for her column. Nothing wrong with creating an incentive for edible complaints and compliments. Except, her charisma was being stretched so thin, even Emily was hard put to get a laugh out of her. Small wonder her students thought they wouldn't get a second chance from her. Else why did practically all of her students keep homework deadlines and a high percentage do extra assignments? Cinder appreciated that her students seemed inspired to their fullest. In her Senior classes, the ship ran so smooth, she had only to navigate. Students did the rowing and the standing at the helm. She wondered if there weren't something special she could do for them. Before she plucked her pillow into her favorite sleep shape, she decided to have them do it. What, she'd think of later. Maybe amongst popover complaints and compliments there would come a plan.

vERN, *who is Ossie to Rachel*

Rachel had flown with him once. Over the green valleys and over big mountains. She had been afraid the whole time. "The wind is so strong, Ossie," she pleaded. "Shouldn't we turn back?"

Vern teased a bit over that. When they hiked the Tumbledown trail in Weld, he teased her about the boulders that made their upward climb more difficult. "Maybe we should turn back, Rachel, before more of these boulders tumble down this path." When he took her fishing on Moose Head Lake, he suggested they should turn back because the fish were so hungry. She seemed to enjoy his teasing her. And she got him a few times. The one he liked best was at Kentucky Fried Chicken in Skowhegan, after they saw Spiderman at the Drive-In. "I don't think we should eat here, Ossie. They cook fingers, you know."

tHE hARRIS fAMILY

"So, how's Len?"

It wasn't a simple question, especially from whence it came. Sally thought it didn't quite fit in with the conversation they'd been having about Dannel's schoolwork. She had been irritated by seemingly kind overtures since the school cookout at the end of the last school year. Several teachers had asked her if she was worried about Len's weight. Sally felt defensive. "Why, sleeping, I suppose."

Ted Crocker gave an "Oh" and finished by reminding her that Dannel's position on the student council depended on his keeping his grades up. "And lately he's been disruptive in meetings. Nothing serious. Just quick on the comments."

Dannel had eaten a peanut butter and jelly sandwich while she was talking to his principal. Sally patted Dannel's broad shoulders, winching from knowing they were that way not because of weight lifting or doing any kind of sports. He was big like his father. She decided to not buy any more jelly or peanut butter. "Are your grades up, Kid?"

"You know they are, Mom. Did Crocker lose something again? They put doors on houses to keep in the heat. I think they should invent doors for teacher's brains to keep in what they say. I pass my work in early. I don't need the extra credit. I just don't like the hassle. From now on, I'm keeping a back up copy for him to sign. I'm bringing that up in the student council. He does it a lot."

"Should your father talk to him?"

"Don't care."

"Listen. I care. Your father had a bad fall down those stairs. Not everyone in the school thinks it was an accident. Some are laughing at him for being a big blubbering bumble that couldn't see the steps and fell on his deserved-ed ass. Crocker really called about him, you know."

Dannel thought it over. "Look, Mom. Don't worry. It must have been a last thought or something. Dad's gonna be back to work soon enough. He didn't fall on purpose. It'll take as long as it takes. Miss Smythe offered to change homerooms. Hers is on the ground floor. He should consider her offer. The sooner he gets back, the better things will be all around."

Sally sat at the table. "Now, about that peanut butter sandwich one hour before supper's ready. That's a no-no. No desert, except fruit or popcorn."

Dannel stood. Patted his mother's shoulder. "Did you notice how our roles changed here?"

"Yes. Who do you think you are, a kid all the time? Grow up and be a lawyer."

"Oh, that reminds me. You gotsta sign a permission paper so I can apply for that Outreach program this summer. I put the paper and the program info on the refrigerator."

"What's on the refrigerator?" Len hobbled into the room and leaned against the table. The smell of simmering stew made him hungry.

"A lock. I'm going to put a lock on it. Now shoo, both of you, so I can finish getting supper."

"Did you call the school to let them know I won't make it in for the In-Service Day?"

"Yes! Now shoo!" Sally stood with one hand on the refrigerator and one holding her pot cover. Feining done, alone in her kitchen, Sally signed the registration form as Dannel had asked. Then she dutifully hid the jar of peanut butter.

fRIEDA

> *Children's stories are filled with pride*
> *Because:*
> *Ant said, "I can't.*
> *Hippo yawned.*
> *Little Engine said, "I can."*
> *Cowboy Sam rode his horse.*
> *Harry Potter flew on a broom.*
> *Crocodile cried crocodile tears.*

Gingerbread Man cried, "You can't catch me!"
And Cow jumped over the moon.

A folded piece of white paper was on the table where only Kevin could have left it. A heart shape drawn in one corner. Two dots and a curved line made it look like a smiling face. Above it was a telephone number. Under it was written "Cinder" underlined three times. Frieda quickly unfolded it to find a recipe. She wondered how involved Cinder was with Kevin's appetite.

The coffeecake came out rather gooey and flat. It was Saturday and Kevin had taken Kade and Dean to the Library. Frieda decided to call the number.

A croaky woman's voice interrupted the friendly voice on the answering machine. "Yes. I'm here."

"It came out flat."

"Wh?"

"The recipe with your phone number on it. Gooey and flat."

"I don't recognize your voice. What recipe?"

"Oh, there were others? The one you gave to Kevin."

"Kevin? Oh, Kevin Young. Muffins. Teachers' room. The muffins were flat?"

"Muffins?"

There was a long pause. "Yes. Excuse me." Frieda heard a coughing sound that threatened not to stop. When it did, Cinder said she had a cold and no chicken soup. She was getting ready to go get some.

"It's raining. You can't go out in the rain with a cough like that. Where do you live?"

"On Crescent. Apollo Apartments. Number three. First floor."

"I know where it is. Unlock your door. Go back to bed. I'm robbing my cupboards of chicken soup and crackers and am on my way. What number?"

She left a note for Kevin beside a plate stacked with coffeecake that should have been muffins. Took two pieces with her.

The door was unlocked. She let herself in. Coughing from the bedroom told her she was in the right place and that Cinder had taken her direction. "I'm here. Be a sec."

She was beautiful. With a red nose and wrapped in an old blanket, she looked the picture of any mother's idea of a grown child on her own in need of chicken soup. Frieda was glad she had made the decision to help this young, sick, but not helpless woman.

Cinder sat down at her kitchen table. Immediately ... but carefully ... attacked the hot soup.

Frieda fished the coffeecake from her bag. "Here. Try these later. They taste great. Must be the recipe."

"Thank you, thank you, thank you, Kevin's wife." Cinder spoke between slurps.

"Cinder. I love the way you're slurping. Reminds me of how Amy and I ate our last Strawberry shortcake. Amy's my boss. At the Anchorage. Plant place. And my best friend. It was a celebration thing."

"It couldn't possibly be as good as this soup," croaked Cinder.

"Whoops. I guess that's my cue to leave you be. Hope you feel better. Rest and liquids. I put some ice cream in your freezer and ginger ale in your fridge. My twins always like to eat soup and ice cream. When you can taste the ice cream, you're getting better. That's a Mom thing."

"Twins? You have twins?"

"Yes. Come meet them, if you like. After you can taste the ice cream."

"Thanks, Mom."

What had Frieda done? Good-neighboring? Amy did it. In her way, Cinder did, too. Frieda felt good to help someone out of kindness. She also felt appreciated.

!W.i.t.h. .o.r. .w.i.t.h.o.u.t. .f.o.r.e.s.i.g.h.t, .F.a.m.i.l.e.s. .c.a.n. .g.r.o.w. .a.n.d. .c.h.a.n.g.e. .t.o.g.e.t.h.e.r!

kEVIN

Kevin paced the floor. Gone to Cinder's? What could she be doing at Cinder's? What business did she have in messing around behind his back? He and the twins had been back an hour. How long had she been gone? He needed to have a beer. If she was any later, he'd have to take the twins and go get some. God, she was inconsiderate. The game would be starting in an hour. She knew he wanted to watch the game. Maybe she would stop for beer to make him feel better about her sneaking over to Cinder's. If she had beer, he wouldn't hassle her over it. Fair was fair.

Frieda shook the rain from her jacket and called to the twins. She had stopped to get pizza, coleslaw, and potato salad.

"Geez, Frieda. You could've gotten beer. Now I gotta go out for it. Put my pizza in the oven so I can have it with the game."

"Sure. We'll eat without you as usual."

"What's that supposed to mean?"

Frieda removed the untouched plate of coffee cake and began to set the table for three. "It means, I don't buy beer. I buy pizza. Oh, good, there's coffee left."

"Well, now that that is settled, why did you go to visit Cinder?"

"She was sick and needed chicken soup."

"That doesn't explain why you went to visit her."

"Because I called the number on the back of the recipe that I thought was coffee cake ... but was muffins ... to see why it came out flat and gooey. I didn't know Cinder was sick until she answered the phone.

Can you imagine, she was about to go out for chicken soup! In the rain! So, I told her to go back to bed and I'd get it. I had to go out for pizza anyway. She feels much better now. Know what, Kade? Know what, Dean? She said, 'Thanks, Mom'."

Kade and Dean took her cue, took turns to thank her for pizza.

"Thanks, Daddy," added Kade and Dean in one voice.

He liked that. It made him turn and look at them. Three faces were turned toward him. Three soft, sensitive faces. His family. "Ha, ha," he managed in a voice he hoped didn't sound fake. "I thank Momma, too. And you're right. That pizza is a great idea, Momma. You guys have convinced me to stay in."

His shift in thought made him feel like having jolly fun with his family, where before he had only felt irritation. He noticed the bright look on Frieda's face. The kids clapped as she put a plate on the table for him. Still, in the back of his mind, was a plan to get beer during halftime. If the game deserved it.

dANNEL

"Listen," he called after her. "I ain't dumb. Just too big on the outside. And that thing you put behind your back is just as bad for you as a candy bar is for me; but a candy bar is legal. That's all I said. That's the way it is and that's ... that's that." His voice trailed off when she turned her dark eyes at him. The force of them stopped his line of thought. He felt helpless. When she turned to continue down the stairs he let his breath leave him slowly. He held onto the railing and watched her body weave amongst students coming up and going down. He had no idea what he was supposed to do next. Or where he was.

aMY

They worked in silence until Amy opened the flood gates. "I love that brother of mine. Grown so big. So strong. You'd never believe he was once a sniveling little whipper snapper who stole my Easter candy."

"Hard to believe how young siblings can tease," agreed Frieda. "Kade and Dean have finally outgrown that."

"Like Kade and Dean, Vern was smart. If he hadn't of been so smart, I'd have been eaten by that bear. Didn't even see the bear coming after the blackberries we were picking. I was singing and stomping out the words to 'Whatcha got cookin'?' Vern stopped picking and I saw the frightened look on his face before I turned to look up. I looked up and up. It was bigger than our Daddy. Smelled bad, too. Vern said, 'Give him your bucket and crawl into the bushes.' Well, I couldn't move any more than let go of them berries I'd picked for my Daddy. I didn't want the bear to get them. 'No, Vern,' I cried. 'Do it,' he whispered. 'He won't eat you if you do.' That was enough for me. I put the bucket on the ground and crawled into the blackberry bushes as far and as fast as I could. Vern reached in and helped me out. I carried him and ran as fast as I could. 'Stop!' Vern whined in my ear. 'I gotta drop my bucket or he'll eat us.' Vern had two buckets. Both full of black, juicy berries. When I got us beyond the berry bushes, I stopped so he could put his small bucket of berries on our path. The bear was coming when I picked him up again. I was used to carrying Vern. He'd get tired on our long walks. In our flight, he never even seemed heavy. 'He's eating them, Amy! He's eating our berries,' Vern whispered in my ear. He could see the bear over my shoulder. I thought it had worked. I thought we were safe. When I got out of breath, Vern made me stop. This time he put his second bucket on the path. Just in case. Good thing. We could hear the bear behind us and couldn't see the house yet. I grabbed his hand and we started to run together. I held on tight because I knew he was getting tired. Then he asked me to stop for breath. 'Amy,' he choked between breaths. 'Take off your sweater. If we give the bear another present, we just might make it home safe.' "

"Well, we did. Vern had saved us both. When our Daddy went to look for my sweater, he came back and picked Vern up and hugged him right close to his heart. Then he hugged me, too. My sweater was torn to bits. The bear had come after us again and stopped to get the berry juice from Vern's bucket off my sweater. Vern saved us by giving the bear four helpings of blackberries. Scout's honor."

Frieda acknowledged, "I always wanted to marry a hero,"

"And you got stuck with a teacher."

"And twins."

"Guess you're the hero."

Again they lapsed into silence. Amy let it stay. Next to the jar of blackberry jam Frieda had prepared for her. It was Frieda's last day and all she could think of was blackberries.

rACINE

Racine Elliot hadn't socialized much since coming to teach at Crossing Place. She thought of it as a temporary environment, one she did not want to get too comfortable with. Cinder Smythe had other plans for her.

"Whatcha doing Racine Elliot?" There seemed more to that question.

"Oh, I'm behind in checking these tests. I really need them finished before next period." Racine supposed that would stall their conversation. It did more than that. Cinder sat right down to help.

"I was wondering if you would like to take tea with me? It's not just with me, really. You see, my friend Emily and I have just finished some quilts we made for people who belong to Wheels on Meals...I mean...Meals on Wheels and we need to, you know, mark them somehow. Inspire the receiver. Our brains are getting fried by Talk Radio. We could use your help. Whaddya say?"

Cinder had talked so fast, Racine stammered, "Well, I usually shop on Tuesday's. The produce is fresher. Did you say Talk Radio? Personally, I avoid it."

"That's how we became friends. Emily and I. Sharing talk radio over the internet. If we didn't have that much in common before, we do now. I'd never thought about making quilts before I met Emily. Come on.

See our lap quilts. Help us design a logo. We won't listen to the radio if you want. Oh, by the way, I don't have a car. Want to give me a ride?"

It was what Racine liked about Cinder Smythe. She wasn't pushy. Just liked to have things her way. Emily seemed that way, too. Racine felt overpowered by the two of them. Emily turned down her radio when Cinder and Racine arrived. The host said something about Saddam Hussein being found before Christmas, or maybe Thanksgiving.

"Whew, that's depressing! Not even funny," said Cinder.

"It's better than saying he couldn't find weapons of mass destruction," countered Emily.

"Or saying why he's really in Iraq," responded Cinder caustically.

"Oops," countered Racine. "You guys are serious."

Emily continued, almost apologetically. "We've got men over there, Racine. And we are worried. We also want to know what is going on over there. And over here. And what the rest of the world knows that we don't. This is one way to do that. The other is C-SPAN. And Free Speech TV with Amy Goodman. Soon Air America will be on the radio. I have high hopes for that. And there are blogs on the net, too. Or we could be a fly on the wall and attend one of those daily briefings. Like before nine eleven."

"And bitter." Racine continued before the two woman had a chance to ask her to butt out. She did not look at them and worked on her design. "I hope you put as much energy into what you plan to do when your men come home. Have you? Or are you just treating an open wound and not looking on the positive side? Sorry, but if your guy dies, do you want your first thought to be 'I told you so?' or 'I will miss you'? Do you keep a scrapbook or a diary? News clips? Anecdotes you want to tell him? You know, what you'd talk about if he were here? Not just what you write about in letters. Well? There's more to do when your man is away than...than... what you can learn from Talk Radio. Find out as much as you can, sure. Don't miss out on your men in the meantime. Anger just doesn't fit in his direction."

Emily seemed appalled. "Well, tell that to my aunt. Do you think it will make her feel better?"

"Yes I do. Not now, but in time. In time for his home coming."

"Why do you say this, Racine?"

Racine stood. "I saw you speak up at our workshop, Cinder. Your face was compassionate and your voice was strong. I was impressed. I wanted to be able to speak up like that. I've always wanted to. I just never really connected, responded to a need. A few hours ago, Cinder, you asked me to join you. And you, Emily, when I first met you, you were listening to music. You don't look like the same people right now. Your eyes are glazed over. Your responses to what you're hearing are quite vulgar. I'm not saying it's wrong; but look in the mirror. See what I see. When I come back, tell me if I'm wrong."

Racine made her way to the bathroom. To use the flush and to splash water on her hot face. She was shaking. She never should have let this side of her show. She had held it in so well. And now ... what was she to do? The room was quiet when she returned to pick up her things. "I'm sorry. I didn't finish ... can't stay. Cinder, if you need a ride tomorrow, I'll come by." She felt their eyes on her. Cinder's and Emily's. She turned to face them.

Emily spoke first. "Your design is great, Racine. We can easily make the rest."

Then Cinder. "Yes. I'd love a ride. Why?"

"It's on my way. I'll be early."

"I meant, I'm sorry we upset you. But why did we?"

Racine could not stop the trembling in her jaw, or the tears that streaked down her cheeks. "He was a long drop of water." The words began to come. So easily now. And she let them. "As stupid as a mule. But he could sing birds out of the trees and charm? He was pure charm. He joined the army to see the world. Gone. Just like that. In Afghanistan. When his letter came. He said it was an odd thing. To be in a place where people seemed afraid of him. He was a good man. And I loved him. He taught me to appreciate nature. He could name every tree, every bird, every wild flower. And draw. My, you'd think his mind made a picture for him to transfer onto paper. Or sculpt with clay. He didn't know why they wanted him to kill people. Before his basic training, he'd never even held a gun.

And nobody ever yelled at him. I wish I could tell him things. Tell him his country loves him. But they don't. They don't care. Not a lick. It's all power play to them. And he's dead. He and other kind souls who were in the wrong place at the wrong time. Trying to make a living. To help his country. To get educated."

"Cripes," moaned Emily. "I hate this. When people hurt and there seems to be no acceptable reason. You're right, Racine. We are caught up. We do care. We want to understand. Sometimes we get sidetracked. But we want to hope. We want to hope, Racine."

Cinder handed Racine a tissue, and took one for herself. "What she said."

"It's the toilet paper," said Racine. "Sean asked a lot of questions about toilet paper. Like, when is a square round? The answer was toilet paper. And what's the last thing to disappear in an empty bowl? Toilet paper!" She wiped at her face. "And things like there's a crisis coming. You're almost out of toilet paper, Emily."

Emily and Cinder stared at Racine, then at each other. Then they were hugging her together with laughter and tears.

"Ouch," said Cinder. "Racine, you made my day. What a fun time that long drink of water must've had in for you. Makes me want to go out and buy toilet paper."

"The next time we get together, let's take in a movie," suggested Emily.

"Good idea, Emily," agreed Cinder. "Or, be jocks and watch a football game."

"Why not fetch some apples? Is there an orchard around here?" Racine felt she might as well find something they could do together. Since she was hooked now.

"Sure," said Emily. "What did you think? We only have potatoes?"

kEVIN

It wasn't a big thing. He'd done it plenty of times before and she'd never said a word. He had to eat, didn't he? She could put less cubed ham in the egg salad. He didn't mind. For some reason Frieda did.

"How much time do you think it would have taken you to cut your own ham or rinse this mustard off the dish, Kevin?" Frieda's words were terse. Rhetorical. Except she must have known he would hear her. He stood behind her and watched her scrape furiously at the dried on mustard.

"Shit, Frieda. Why get upset over a little thing like that?"

Frieda gripped the side of the sink. She wiped her hands with a dish towel. "No, there's more. You'd better sit down, Kevin."

Kevin felt more curiosity than concern. He could give her that. After all, the kids were at their grandmother's. Maybe she just had the jitters and needed a break.

Frieda sat at the kitchen table. She opened a large envelope that was addressed to her and took out some papers. "I don't know how to tell you, Kevin. I've tried to find the right time. When you didn't have a big thing at school or wasn't drinking or we had just eaten or Kade and Dean . . . ." Frieda let her voice trail off.

"Christ, Frieda. There's no reason to get all theatrical. I'll just get a beer."

"No. Sit. Just sit." Her voice was sharp.

His curiosity left him. He felt the familiar irritation he often felt around Frieda.

"There's something wrong with me. I need an operation. I have cancer."

Just like that she told him this? From mustard to cancer? He had steeled himself to hear a tirade of what he had been doing wrong and she stiffs him with this? "Where? What kind of cancer? Christ, Frieda. Christ." His irritation ebbed to fear. "How do you know?"

"I've had tests. I've done the research. I've tried special diets. It's all here. Among these papers. I found a lump in my left breast. I called Doctor Eiser right away. The mammogram showed lumps in both breasts. He sent me to Bangor for tests. The biopsy came back malignant. There's no chance to do anything else now, but to operate. I am scheduled for a double mastectomy in ten days. I'm so sorry. I am so afraid. I didn't want to worry you. Then I didn't know how to tell you."

He swore. He looked at her papers. "Double? Christ, Frieda. You've known this for weeks! How could you not tell me?" For a moment, he half expected to hear some excuse from her. An apology. What kind of a heel was he? She was his wife! The mother of his twins. He loved her. He didn't want her hurt like that. Even if he'd known sooner, the cancer was not going away by itself. He wished he had that beer. He wished he'd been there for her. Then he closed the space between them. She clung to him as he held her. He could feel her heart beating against him. He forgot about the beer. All he wanted was Frieda. He wanted her to know that. "I want you, Frieda," he whispered. "I want you so much. Please, Frieda. I love you so much."

Neither of them held back. They made love with grunts and thrusts and laughter and sweat. They came together. They clung together. They came together once more.

When she awoke, Kevin was looking at her. "You're beautiful, Frieda. I'd almost forgotten." He slipped down beside her.

"I'm a coward, Kevin. I wrote letters to you and the twins. I was so angry then. I blamed your drinking for my unresponsiveness. Not the lumps. I did not understand the consequences at first. I didn't want to go through with it. I wanted to scream and run into traffic. Don't look so alarmed. I love my life. I love who I am. I love being married to you. And having our twins. I don't want you to hate me. To be angry at me. I'm sorry it took me so long to realize that."

"OK. I'll just blame you." Kevin deadpanned his voice and looked his eyes up at her from his down turned head.

"Kevin, that is the funniest thing you could have said. That is why I love you. I love your jokes."

She was right. He used to joke. He liked to hear her laugh.

"Who else knows?"

"I told Amy first. Then my mother. And now you."

He let it go. "Girl talk. Always amazes me. Speaking of such, we should be thinking about a live in housekeeper. Starting as soon as we can find one. While you are able to take charge. You'll be very sick, Frieda. For a long time. I'd hate for you to suffer more than you already are. Will." He could not think that she could die from this.

"I'll be disfigured. So ugly. You always loved my breasts."

"Now that's not funny. Don't go there, Frieda. This is happening to both of us. I'm a history teacher, remember? And a family man. I'll always remember how turned on I used to get when I saw your breasts holding up that pink sweater you wore as a cheerleader. That was months before our first real date. So what do you think?"

Her eyes became very big. He thought she was going to cry again. "Can I get you something pink?"

She cried then. He engulfed her from his heart to his toes.

"What's done is done," he told her. "You never know what you will do under stress. What thousands of people under the same stress will do. So don't worry that you couldn't tell me right away. We have a few weeks. We can do a lot in a few weeks. We can even not do a lot."

Behind his words came his own confession. How could he have been so blind? It was not something he was proud of. He made a silent vow to refrain from drinking. He no longer had the stomach for it.

aMY

Chill from last night's frost lingered around her perennial garden long after the fog had lifted above the lakes and sunrise highlighted the crisp Autumn colors. Amy specifically noticed the crisp colors of each autumn sunrise as she opened her shop. Monarch butterflies were gone now. It must have been the hurricane that came ashore off the Carolina coast and pushed North through New York state that delayed them. That and days of warm rain. Would probably rain later today. She was in good spirits as usual as she signed for a delivery of long stemmed roses and Spring bulbs. There'd be a rush on those bulbs today. Before customers came in, she hurried to arrange the roses in cold storage. She had to leave the bulbs on their cellophane wrapped pallets until help arrived. That help did not include Frieda.

"Excuse me, could you tell me if I should plant Spring bulbs in the Fall?"

Amy was quick. "Of course! Plant Spring bulbs in the Fall, or fall behind in the Spring. Got it? The ground, you know. Freezes?"

The young customer laughed. "I feel so silly. Of course! I need about thirty. All one color. I want my students to plant them. I like blue. Or white. Or yellow."

Amy was surprised that this little waif of a thing was a full grown teacher. "Students? Excuse me, do you often surprise those that judge you by your cover?" She couldn't help being blunt. This woman seemed not to mind. She was also blunt.

"I teach Literature and Fine Arts at the High School. My name's Cinder Smythe. You must be Amy. You have a reputation when it comes to students. They adore you. They say if there's anyone in this old town that understands them, it's Amy-Over-At-the-Greenhouse. Why, that tall girl, Ellen Fowler, wrote about the time you threw fertilizer at big kids who were beating up on little kids. You told them to go home and grow up. I gave her an A+ for that story. You look much like that illustration Ellen made for it. What kind of fertilizer did you use?"

"Only the best. Clumps of rich horse shit. Great for helping to get bushy plants off to a healthy start."

Cinder clapped her hands together in a fit of laughter. "No wonder the kids laughed at Ellen's story. They knew! I must tell Rudd about that one. He's 'Raqing, you know. As a National Guard soldier. I guess there are more National Guard units in Iraq from Maine than any other state. Some get parceled off to beef up other state units. It just blows my mind; but I'm not about to pine away just because I'm waiting to hear how and when my Rudd is coming home."

Amy thought she instinctively knew where Cinder Smythe's words were going. "Hm! You know, there's this column in the Bangor paper? It's sort of a sounding board, plays on words, a starting point to work through problems. The Country Chaty-ant. She has a way of laying out one thing that could be another. You might find them soulful." Amy was surprised to learn otherwise.

Cinder burst into tears. "Thank you. I'm sorry," she managed to say between moping at her tears. "I won't hide this from you. No one else knows, Amy. If you don't want to keep it undercover, I won't hold it against you. It's just that what you said about the Country Chaty-ant touches me right to the quick. I'm a writer, you see. I've written stories all my life. Sometimes just for myself and for my Rudd. I wrote for my college newspaper. Then I got so caught up in the negative news from the Right Wing media, I began a positive feedback type column. It was so popular, it was picked up by the Bangor paper. I'm the Country Chaty -ant. I call it *Shaw-toy-awnt*."

Amy let Cinder Smythe's words sink in as casually as they were offered. "So that's how it works. I got no problem with keeping that undercover. I got an immediate problem. My co-workers are all off being sick and I gotta unwrap all these bulbs by myself. Why don't you give me a hand while you tell me more about this guy Rudd? We gots to say our thoughts out loud sometimes. It helps the flowers grow."

"Is that another ... you know ... fertilizer story?" Asked Cinder, tugging on garden gloves.

fRIEDA

It happened again.
The belligerent putdowns.
One way conversation.
Boxed in mind set.
Ready for confrontation.
Face, contorted with exaggerated expression,
placed close to mine.
Torso to torso, your breath warm against my nose.
I wonder if you are planning
to throw me into the dishwasher.

I could give in.
I could go get what you want.
But I want you to be sober more.
If it were me, wouldn't you want that?

Frieda was firm about his slipping. "It's not that it is just one more time, Kevin. It's that we have things to get through together, and this is one of them."

He stared at her for a long time, as though trying to hold his throbbing head so the muddle in his brain would not erupt. "It's one of those things that's gotten to me. I'll be alright, Frieda. This time was different. I know it didn't help. I don't know if that's enough for me to stop. I want it to be."

Frieda watched the look on his face turn from helpless to hard and back again. "Your family is another reason, Kevin."

"Then I guess I will have to stop."

Even these words did not please Frieda. "Just say you will. You know there's no guessing. Want to, you can. Want to, you will. It hurts to see you change from it. When Kade and Dean see you like that. I love you, Kevin. And I know it's not enough unless you want it, too."

Frieda left him standing there amongst the kitchen clutter as she whisked the twins away to Day Care. Had Kevin known it was her last testing session before her operation, he may have offered to be with her. Her Mother was going with her and Frieda planned to confess about Kevin's drinking. About why he had stayed behind so much. She knew it was not so terrible of her to try to keep it quiet. She had hoped for it to get better. His choice made her angry. She could see that now. She could no longer hide what she felt. Her need for her Mother's understanding was stronger than her need for Kevin's love. She no longer felt it was her duty to protect him in his downturn. As though she were breaking a trust. She began to have confidence in these feelings after Amy got her to write a letter to *The Country Chatoyant* column in the Bangor paper. The answer was spiced with humor and advise and quoted comments. From other women who faced similar predicaments. It was a bunch of things to Frieda. ***"Nothing is simple in this*** *world,"* began the column. ***"You think you've found the missing handle for one thing, and there's a flat tire on it."*** In the middle it said, ***"Know what? You're not the only one who's dialed that same number."*** And it ended with, ***"When the kettle boils, it's time to take off the lid or turn down the heat. Let me know if that lid trick works for you."***

Frieda wondered what her Mother would say of that lid. Throw it at Kevin?

eLLEN

"Ellen, it's not a boy friend," called out Sammy.

Ellen's mother, Ruby Mitchell, motioned at him to be silent. Sent him to watch TV. Led the man in the rumpled blue shirt to her kitchen table. Handed him a glass of water.

Ellen, always spontaneous and inquisitive, followed them to the kitchen table. "What's wrong, Mr. Young?"

Kevin began slowly, looking from Ellen to her mother. "I don't know how to ask about this, Mrs. Mitchell...Ruby. Ellen. I feel like I might be intruding or something. So I'll just say it straight out. I need help. It's my wife, you see. She needs an operation. She's going to be quite sick afterwards. And I got these two kids. They go to daycare, but I need someone to care for them when I'm at the hospital and when I'm working and can't be there. And to clean and cook. I'm not good at either of them. When she comes home she'll need someone to help her. Len Harris told me of you."

"Mr. Harris. That old blimp? Thinks I can help you out? Maybe so. Ellen, too. We could use some extra money, what with Ellen fixing to go to college and all."

"I'll be straight, too," said Ellen in her crisp, young voice. "You drink, don'tcha, Mr. Young? Do you drink around the kids? Can you stop that if your wife is sick? Cause if you can't, you may as well bark up a different tree."

"Ellen," corrected Her Mother. Then to Kevin Young, "Explain, please."

He looked straight at Ellen. "I stopped. I hope I can stay stopped. Frieda's trouble is a strong incentive for me to stop. I have slipped once. Frieda caught me. I won't forget the way she looked at me. It's enough to make a man feel unproud, I can tell you."

"Well, OK then. What you think, Momma?"

"We can work something out. You need us. We can help. No choice. Right, Ellen?"

"Sure. You know Amy Shirly? She would see it that way."

"Then we can help you, Mr. Young. There is this one other thing you must tell us. Names. Give us names and a list of special things we should know. And we must begin to visit right away. Ellen should walk with your wife and the twins as much as she can. You know, be around. I can start cooking right away. It will be fun. And what about Sammy?"

"There's private rooms. You use what you need. It's up to you. You can move in or keep up this place." He paused. "I'd really like for you to move right in and take over just as you do now. No offense. I want you to know I'm a family man, Mrs. Mitchell. Ruby. I respect your family, too. Whatever you think is best."

"So now we have two things to do, Ellen. See these rooms he talked about and see if my cooking is good enough for his family."

"And be sure there is more than one TV," added Sammy, who had come quietly into the room and sat across the table from Ellen's teacher and next to his mother who poured him a glass of water.

Ellen spoke then. "That first week can begin anytime, Mr. Young. Depends. We don't move in until the twins and Mrs. Young accept us. You pay the arrangements for us to move. We get a contract as to what is expected and how we can do that. How we get paid, food, time off, privacy, tutoring."

"Tutoring?"

"Sammy has trouble in history."

"You can bribe him with jello," laughed her mother. She took some helpings of it from the refrigerator for Mr. Young and Sammy. "We add fruit juice to make a healthy treat. The recipe is on the box."

Mr. Young seemed amazed by the composition and taste. "You've got my attention. The twins will love you immediately. Friends for life!"

Ellen's Mother chuckled. "Thank you. First we must meet the family, Mr. Young. Then we can talk over what Ellen suggested. Yes? You have a nice night, now, Mr. Young. We have no phone. I will wait for you to leave a message with Ellen."

Ellen saw Mr. Young to the door and shook his hand.

rUBY

Ruby was elated. "Ellen. Sammy. You wanna do this thing for a TV and a nicer place to stay? And be paid for it, too?'

Seconds later, all three were laughing, deciding what they would take with them. Mr. Young's problem could be the blessing they'd prayed for.

fRIEDA

The white horse had wheels where it touched the floor.
The floor was carpeted with white and surrounded by walls
The walls were outlined with lights that shone in my eyes.
I followed them until the man in the blue cloth hat said my name.
Then a man and a woman lifted me from my horse to a table.
They, too, wore blue cloth hats.
As I lay there, they poked needles into my arms.
They told me I would soon be asleep.
They promised to keep me warm.
Then my name was called in a quiet, strange way.
I thought of Kade. I thought of Dean.
I thought how Daddy would hug them at bedtime.
I pretended I was there to hug them, too.
I pretended they were wearing blue hats.
I pretended they rode upon my white horse.
And Kade asked

"Why does the horse have wheels, Momma?"
And Dean asked,
"Will the horse ride us to sleep, Momma?"
And Daddy answered for me because I was asleep.
"Wheels are quiet, Kade," said Daddy.
"It's easier to ride to sleep on a wheeled white horse, Dean,"said Daddy.
"Like Mommy?" asked Kade and Dean.
"Like Mommy," answered Daddy.
"Thanks, Mommy." I heard Kade and Dean say in one voice.
And then I heard a horse gallop into the sunset.
"Thanks, Daddy," said Dean and Kade in one voice.
And they each added thanks to Ruby and Sammy and Ellen.
"And Billy," said Dean and Kade bumping each other's noses. Somewhere in the pasture among the wildflowers,
the horse stopped to rest.
Knowing all were there together, all safe, helped me sleep.

rUBY

Tears streamed down Ruby's cheeks as she read Frieda's words and looked at the family pictures Frieda had arranged in one book for Dean and one book for Kade. At the blank pages where more could be added.

"Yes," she said in her kind, mothering voice. "You have done it. Asleep alive. Asleep not. Either way. It is done. It is good."

Frieda nodded silently. Her smile showed her thanks for Ruby's support.

"I wish I could have done something like this for my children."

"When you lost their father?"

"And their mother."

"I don't understand."

"Frieda. Not all families start together. Some grow together. As my Ellen has with me. As our Sammy has, too. I wish I could make a book about our family. Growing together."

She felt Frieda's hand upon her shoulder. "I declare, Ruby. If you can think it, it's half done!"

fRIEDA

Frieda had expected to see them all waiting for her when she awoke. Her family. Her extended family. Silly lady. She came to in quite a state. All groggy and sick like. She did not feel her chest. She knew the damage had been done to her. She actually did not want to move. "What time is it?" She tried to ask. Her mouth felt stiff because of the tube that must have been there.

Someone put a wet sponge to her lips. "No water, yet, young lady. How do you feel?"

"Horrible," Frieda tried to say.

"You are in recovery, Frieda. It's about time you woke up. There are a handful of people who will be glad they can go home now. Now that you are awake, they can get some sleep. Do you want to see your husband?"

"Yes." Frieda's voice was stronger. "Cover me."

And a warm blanket was tucked around her. And Kevin's voice whispered, "Ready?"

Sometimes we see people again for the first time. Frieda now understood those *Chatoyant's* words when Kevin strode proudly toward her. He looked tired and brave and strong. Just for her! "Thanks, Daddy," she whispered. She tried not to laugh too hard when Kevin said, "Thanks, Momma. You might not feel like it, but to me, you are the greatest looking Momma on this earth!"

That's what Frieda heard. The rest would have to be repeated later. What the doctor had told him and what she could now expect. Frieda had more rest to do first.

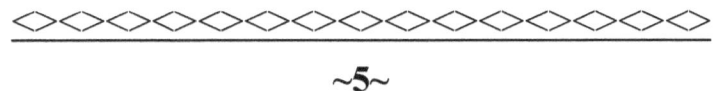

~5~

!O.f.f. w.e. g.o, n.o.w, t.o. w.h.e.r.e. m.o.r.e. o.f. t.h.e p.e.o.p.l.e. i.n. C.r.o.s.s.i.n.g. P.l.a.ce. .s.e.e.m. .l.i.k.e. .h.e.r.o.e.s!

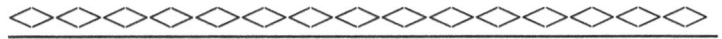

tHE hARRIS fAMILY

Sally sat on the edge of the couch where she could listen to the sound of the family car over the drone of the television. It wasn't like Dannel to take so long. She worried that something had happened. No. He'd call. She was wasting good energy. She got up to check the weather. By the time she sat down again, headlights shone in the window. Sally slid back into the pillows then. She should know that things would always work out.

The knock on the door spoke otherwise.

She was at the door before Len got out of his chair. She glanced over at him to be sure he had his crutches before she pulled open the door.

Officer Robert Fly stood with his cap in hand.

Sally gasped.

Fly asked if he could come in.

Len reached her side.

Other car lights came into the drive.

Sally turned from the door to hide her face against Len.

Fly said it had been snowing some.

Another man entered the house and brushed past Fly. "'Cuse me," he said in a familiar voice.

Sally lifted her face from Len's shoulder to demand of her son, "Where have you been? You should have been back an hour ago."

"Hey, Mom! I'm back. I gotta admit that Officer Fly is some driver when he's being tailed by a teenager. What kind of fuel do you burn in order to keep your engine from stalling when it runs so slow?"

"Is that all you wanted, Fly?"

"Well, no, Sally. I'm on highway duty down the road. When it started to snow, I began hankering for a cup of hot chocolate. And I said to myself, 'Sally's place is a sight nearer than Dicker's Corner.' And I wonder if you might'n have a cup to spare?"

"To spare?" Sally felt like giving him a cup of chocolate alright. In a month of Sunday's! But she held her tongue. "OK, big brother. Big brother Bob Fly. Come in and sit down. I'll see what I can do for an officer who's on highway duty and comes in to scare the mother of a driver half to death! And it ain't snowing, Bob! I no more than two minutes ago looked out that there window and didn't see one flake of snow."

"The snow's out there and coming down, Sally. Tell her, Dannel."

"Further down, in town, Mom. There's rain coming down. It might turn to snow by the time you get that cocoa going. The man's gotta have his cocoa."

Sally noticed a rip in Dannel's right front pocket as he casually brushed past her toward the stairway to his room. "Dannel?" she called in her best mother voice. "Did you forget the groceries?"

"Nope. On the table." His voice floated done cheerfully. As though he always placed groceries on the table and did not bother to put them away. As though she always asked.

sAMMY

Sammy closed his eyes; but images of bloody zippers on Mrs. Young's chest were still there. She had left the bathroom door ajar as she splashed water on her face. Her robe was open so she could look at herself in the mirror. She just stood there and cried. Ever so quietly. Sammy wanted to cry, too! What had they done to her? He knew she had not seen him. He wished he had not seen her. He made himself remember what he liked about her. How good she was to him. How she didn't mind that he was slow and stupid. She made him laugh at himself and promise to "Stop acting like a volcano, for heaven's sake!" When Mrs. Young came home from the hospital, she said she was the one who was slow and stupid. She said she was working hard at getting better like he was working hard in thinking before he did something 'out of context' or got him into trouble. She said they could help each other.

Sammy thought Mrs. Young must be the bravest person he knew! Momma told Ellen that the doctor wanted to sew in some jelly so Mrs. Young would have something there to hold her blouse up. Ellen said all she needed was a padded bra. He knew about those. Girls in his Freshman class wore them.

That night, Sammy dreamed of a classroom filled with girls in padded bras and Mrs. Young was one of them. Only she was smiling and telling him he was brave, too. He forgave himself for innocently trespassing on Mrs. Young. His dream was a dry one.

sALLY

It was a little thing. Sally almost let it go. Had she done that, the drama that began that night may have affected her son differently.

Len had a cup of cocoa with Bob. Sally climbed the stairs and walked softly toward Dannel's room. A voice, antagonistic and threatening, did not sound like her son's.

"This is not the way it goes, see! Kick ass? I'll tell you who can kick ass. Make no mistake about that."

Sally heard a thump. Was someone in Dannel's room?

"What you gonna tell? I should have left you there? I'm to blame for your being messed up? Which year are we talking about? Seems to me, you haven't learned what you should've figured out in Kindergarten! That's it. Take no aspirin and don't call me in the morning! In fact, don't call me in your life!"

The voice stopped. Sally stood staring at Dannel's door. When she knocked, her mother's heart let her adult head take charge.

"Yeah?" Dannel's voice was falsely sleepy.

"In coming. Make yourself ready."

He was sitting on the edge of his bed holding his phone. Tears streaked his cheeks. His schoolbooks were on the floor. Sally sat down beside him and put her arm around his shoulders. "I guess we need to talk," she said softly. "I was standing outside your door, Dannel. Please talk to me about it."

"I really don't want to."

"I know. Start with a name."

"I really .... "

Sally waited.

"Crocker. Okay? Biggest jerk in the world of girls!"

Sally held her tongue. Her mother's heart felt for him.

"You came to ask me about being late getting back, didn't you? Well, there was this reason. I couldn't help it. She made me forget what I was doing. She makes me forget to breathe. I thought I was helping her. I saw what she was doing and I just tried to reason with her. I won't try to any more." Dannel's voice was shaky. He reached for his jacket. "See this? Not a big thing. It could've been my head. Marley was in the store and asked for a ride to her friend's house. There were three cars parked in the driveway. All friends of Marley's. All losers as far as I'm concerned. I decided not to stop. Marley pulled and jabbed at me. She screamed at me to let her out. She called me names. Tore my jacket. So I let her out alright. In her own driveway. Her parents just got home from somewhere and thanked me for giving her a lift. So I told them where she wanted to go and why I did not stop and brought her home. I always thought Crocker was dense. Mrs. Crocker ... well ... she had the same look you have on your face right now."

"Right. My son does the responsible thing and I have a funny look on my face."

"It's a wise look, Mom. Do you think you can mend this rip?"

"The rip. I can always do good at rips. Let's see what there is you can say about Marley's problem first."

Dannel sat quietly. His shoulders slumped toward his chest. Sally guessed he did not know what it was she wanted. "What I want is for you to know what to do about the problems you've noticed about Marley, and what to do about the problems Marley's caused for you."

"Duh, Mom. Aren't they the same thing?"

"No. And I wish I could let you sleep on it." She went to the door and looked at her son. "I'm changing your curfew. No free use of car as of now. I'm not sure that your decision to drive Marley to a party was a good one." She held up her hand. "I know. You actually took her home; but that was a second choice. We can talk later about that first thought. I'm on my way downstairs. Is there an address I could talk to Fly about?"

Dannel showed an uneasiness. He shook his head.

"I see. Is that a code of some kind? It's not a good one, but that's your choice. I'm betting on the Mother Code." Sally blew him a kiss and closed his door.

cROCKER'S

"Wait just a minute, young lady. What friends were that Harris boy talking about?"

"They're just friends from school, Mother."

"Friends with cars. Did you plan to get a ride in all three of them?"

"No, silly. They were parked."

"Don't call your mother silly. Parked where?" Crocker was angry

"You know, parked."

"Together." Crocker deserved her dead end answer.

"Yes, together."

"Have you been there before?" Jayne Crocker had had enough.

"Yes. Lotsa times. I don't appreciate Dannel's teasing me like that."

"He didn't sound like he was teasing to me." Mrs. Crocker spoke clearly.

Ted Crocker said something under his breath before heading for the bathroom.

Jayne Crocker thought Dannel had said what she should have known. "Marley, I don't want you hanging out in stores looking for rides to parties. In fact, I don't want you to go to parties unless I know where you are going, how you are getting there, and who will be there. I expect you to be in earlier from now on."

"Oh, no. I didn't do anything wrong. Dannel's the one wrong here."

"Eight o'clock on school nights. Nine o'clock on other nights. If you have a problem with that, appeal to your father in the morning. I'd like you to go to your room now. Good night, Marley." Mrs. Crocker's head hurt. When Marley walked away, Mrs.Crocker wrote the new curfew on a pad of paper so she could remember in the morning. Mrs. Crocker thought something was wrong with that picture. In the mirror, she saw her half closed eyes. Behind her, she noted the unsteady steps of Mr. Crocker.

She and Ted seemed to have so much to offer Marley. She felt now that they were failing. Before she went to bed, Jayne Crocker thought of ways to communicate with Marley, to spend more time with her. If only Mrs. Crocker and Ted were happier like they were when Marley was a beautiful infant with dark curls and the joy to their hearts. If only Marley could understand that circumstances between her parents were difficult now. Since Mrs. Crocker stopped feeling well and Ted's son left home.

mARLEY

Her mother did not have a clue! *Do this, Marley. Do that, Marley. Why don't you bring your friends over? Oh, why didn't you tell me about that, Marley? I would have liked to have gone with you.* As if she hadn't tried a thousand times to get her mother interested in what she was doing. *Now don't fret, Marley. I'm going to lie down for awhile. If your father calls, tell him to pick something up for supper. You can call for a pizza, if you want. There's money in my purse.* It was so easy to take the money. Her mother never asked her about it. Her father didn't seem to care one way or the other. Except when he wanted something. *What about those grades, Marley? Don't look for an allowance from me until they get better. If you want to spend your time eating pizza instead of studying, the consequences will be on your shoulders!* Marley didn't need to study. She got by without it. She never ordered pizza, either. She wouldn't get fat. Ever! If she ate too much, all she had to do was purge. It made the highs seem much better. There was plenty ways to get high. Tonight she wasn't that lucky. Dannel had blown that for her. Well, she told him off but good. He'd never offer to help her again. She never should have called him back. He was a creep but always helped her out of fixes before. What had he said? In my life? In your life? Marley sobbed under her pillow. She did not understand why Dannel's words were more important to her than her mother's. She had nothing to help her stop the hurt and confusion she was feeling. Not even Dannel. He called her a slut. Was she a slut? Right when she needed his help the most, he turned his back on her. He'd been her best friend since they were play partners in kindergarten! How could he be so cruel?

vERN

"Coming in the front door," he cracked in his loud, commanding voice. Amy didn't need to look. Vern always announced himself as if she needed to be forewarned. As if she had her hand in the cookie jar. "Where's Amy?"

He found her in the potting shed. "You got two dozen red roses?"

"Depends. For a girl or a boy?"

"For a lady. She's a fine lady. I want to surprise her."

"A lady. Would the lady like yellow tea roses?" Amy removed her potting gloves very carefully and placed them beside her bucket.

"No. She would like red roses."

"I've got some beautiful white roses."

"Are you hard of hearing, girl? Red. Long stemmed red roses."

"Oh, long stem. You sound serious."

"Yep. You gotta remove the thorns. Special request."

"Who's this special lady, Vern? Two dozen long stemmed de-thorned roses is a lot of attention...even for a lady."

"Don't worry, Amy. She's so special, I don't even need a card."

Amy smiled. "Like I said, special attention."

He wondered if she knew. She knew everybody's business. He admired her that.

rACHEL

Rachel's attire was immaculate. Her red painted fingernails had no chips. Her long black hair had only a few tendrils out of place. Her step was as sure and steady as when she stood barefoot on the black horse's back and rode him around the corral. She didn't think of those times as much now. Times when she had to do stunts like that to earn money. Unless her belt rubbed painfully across her scar, did she remember how desperate her family had been to come to America. It was a deep cut. From the broken glass in the window her father used to get into the rich man's house to steal his things. She had been the lookout. When she saw the man coming along the path, she ran to the window to warn her father just as he came crashing back through. She thought she was dead. So much blood. Her father pulled the broken glass from her body and wrapped her into the large white sack along with his loot. The man came and helped carry her to the woods to a hidden shack where a woman smothered her cut with ashes from the fire. The pain made her want to scream, but she was too afraid of the man who stood watching her. Her mother came and washed her face with a red cloth. The man finally spoke. Rachel could not make out the words. Then her mother was hugging the man's feet. What would happen to her father? Was the man going to kill him? Then her mother came again to wash her face with the red cloth. "You are very brave, Rachel. The man said such a brave child deserves to live. He took back what your father stole from him. He has given us money to go to America. We will fly in a big plane all the way to At Lanta. Your brothers. Your sisters. Your mother. Your father. We will all go to America. Only, you need to get well. Then we go."

Rachel's mother called the purplish tissue that was left from the cut across her belly her American Rainbow. Scars on her temple could be hidden with her hairstyle. "Do not worry," her beautiful sisters had told her. "A man can love you in spite of your scars. You won't need to hide them if he loves you. You'll see." She had not believed them. She felt she was doomed to martyrdom among her family.

Until Ossie hugged her. The day it rained and they went bird sighting. When they had burst ... wet and laughing ... together into her family home. When she introduced Vern to her family as Ossie. "I mean, Vern. Ossie is his sighting bird."

"Welcome to our casa, Vern," said her papa. "We have food. Let's eat." And then, around food, the meal was not a quiet one, yet Ossie filled a spot in the conversation with a story about flying over a frozen lake and seeing snow angels. And since it was still raining and they had left their cars at the restaurant, Rachel's father drove them to their cars. On the way, Ossie said he had a great time and wanted to see her again.

"You know where to find me, Ossie," she'd told him.

"Yeah, I do. I feel like I've known you for a long time."

"Longer than I've had your book."

"Right. I'm sure glad you found that book."

"Si." She wanted him to hug her again. She hoped it would be soon.

In her bird book she listed the man she liked for his bigness and gruff voice under Osprey. As Ossie. She called him that because he flew planes. She called him by that name when they were alone. He made her feel like flying when they were alone. She supposed she'd even fly through windows for him.

Rachel felt even stronger on that now, as she dashed down the stairs as soon as she heard Ossie's car turn into the driveway. Why did her heart tremble so? Did she think he would forget?

"Vern asked me to make this," said her mother as she handed Rachel a parcel.

It smelled good. She was happy to take it.

vERN, *who is Ossie to Rachel*

Rachel was a trooper. She'd learned how to pack parachutes and often came to help clean his plane. He always found time to be with her, even if he was busy in his charter business. He and Rachel were long overdue for another air trip. "On the next sunny day, when you take a day off, I'm going to show you something as great as snow angels. Something so beautiful, it'll make you want to fly forever."

There'd be no turning back this time. He was ready to stake his life on it. When he saw her rushing out of her house to meet him, he had no doubt that she felt the same way.

aMY

It had rained some. Probably would rain off and on all weekend. Amy thought about the winds and Vern's flying off into the sunset with his special order of roses and a very special lady. Who would that be, she wondered. What available lady would be hanging around this old town? Then she chided herself. She was available. Just thirty-two in April, she was no Delta Dawn.

Amy took her plate to her sink and stacked it as carefully as she had her breakfast dishes. She would wash them later. She had to get to her oil painting. It was the largest one she had tried. Perhaps her best.

Once, when Vern had asked, she told him she saw value in seeking pleasure in personal accomplishments, no matter how small. She told him their father always said luck depended on the attitude one generated around themselves. She never tried to force that attitude. She did her best to plant it. One plant at a time. Plus a little fertilizer and a lot of watering.

That was the pluck her father had left to her. That and enough money for her to start her greenhouse. Pluck for her to raise Vern and see that he got to college. Pluck to beg for scholarships and to accept those that had no visible stings attached. This pluck kept her going after her husband left with their child when she was having a mastectomy. "That there fella that married you, run off," Vern told her. "Papa went after him. Found him, too. Him and baby Niomi. She was wearing the sweater set you made for her. Papa couldn't talk any sense into him. Papa says you better get well so's you can go after them yerself. Papa came back all tired and looking like an old man. He's real sick."

Who'd have guessed Vern would learn to fly like a bird? Who'd have guessed she'd never get her child back? Married, deserted, and divorced by seventeen. Amy touched the locket she wore on a golden chain above her heart. Her wedding ring hung there, too. Vern once teased her about not having enough pluck to wear them in the open. She reminded him she had the pluck alright. She didn't need to validate her past to anyone but herself. Anyways, it was more pride than pluck.

vERN

The fall foliage took Rachel's breath away. "You are right, Ossie. This must be as beautiful as snow angels. Maybe we can do those later. Si, Ossie?"

"Si, mon petite." He winked at her from his pilot's seat. The roses she held against her white dress gave her an awesome look. Like the feeling he held in his heart for her. The feeling he would soon be sharing with her. Before or after they ate the lunch Rachel's Mother had packed for them. He also had plans for the roses.

rACHEL

Ossie was right. Rachel was thrilled by the foliage below her. She looked at Ossie and saw the same excitement in his face that she felt. The face of a man she trusted in her heart. Somewhere between the sky and landing on the lake, she felt as one with him. She knew she loved him. And she was afraid.

After they secured his Bi-plane to the dock and before hiking to the small cabin, Ossie skipped rocks across the sun's reflection in the lake. She clapped excitedly each time the bouncing rocks made sparkling ripples of light. Then they took their supplies to the small cabin.

"I'm hungry," said Ossie. "S'pose you take care of that while I take care of the roses."

Of course he kissed her first. And left a tingle of a lingering hug upon her arms. Rachel set about her task at once. She was lighting the candles when he returned. He placed small glasses of water beside each plate. In each there was a rose. He had cut the stem so it would fit and not tip over.

The meal Rachel's mother had prepared for them was eaten amidst laughter and stories. Soon they sat before a magnificent fire in the fireplace. Wrapped close together in a colorful Indian blanket.

"Ossie, I am feeling so fine. It's like the feeling I had when I stood upon the black horse and rode him around the coral so the buyer could see how gentle he was. I felt like one with him. I felt like I could ride him like that forever. I feel like that now, Ossie."

"Rachel, Rachel, Rachel." His kiss was so sweet. It brought them to their feet. It lasted as they slipped from their clothes and made ready for bed.

"Ossie, we can't sleep here! There's these things in our bed!"

He lit the candles so she could see.

Now Rachel felt a loss of words. Ossie had spread the rest of the roses upon the bed. He took her hand and together they jumped amongst them. Tossed them at each other. She felt such joy. She gave herself to him passionately. Like she never thought possible. Like she was a beautiful goddess without flaws or horrid past. Like it was to be! In a bed of roses.

And there was more.

Ossie asked her to marry him.

And Rachel said, "Yes!"

jAYNE cROCKER

There was no response to her knock. Mrs. Crocker opened the door anyway. "It's late, Marley. Your breakfast and lunch are in the microwave."

Marley was not in the room. Her bed was made. In fact, the room looked neat except for the open closet door. That in itself could have made Mrs. Crocker smile: but Mrs. Crocker couldn't remember if Marley had come home the night before or stayed with friends. Mrs. Crocker made a mental note to find out the names of Marley's friends.

cINDER

Out of the classroom, students let down their guard. Cinder knew this from the graveyard trip. But here, in the arc of green facing the school walkway, planting blue and white spring bulbs in the pattern laid out by Ellen, the Seniors were talking politics with an atmosphere of heightened anxiety.

"Just because I'm eighteen, I could be yanked right out of my life and sent to fight a war in a place where someone could be saying, 'Duck!' and I think they mean 'Fuck!' "

"What do you mean? There's no draft. Just say 'No!' "

"I'm still trying to figure out where the terrorists are. Did they all flee to Iraq when we bombed Afghanistan?"

"Even I know the difference between Iraq and Afghanistan."

"When in doubt, who you going to bomb? I get it, Iraq. They can pay us off in oil."

"You don't get it. This is about human rights and weapons of mass destruction."

"Ain't gonna do much good if your head is blown off."

"You wanta go over there and be killed because your government was so hell bent for war they forgot to give you the proper gear?"

"Our president says they are evil."

"Well, the UN said they would not support that."

"Support what?"

"Us going into Iraq."

" Yeah, and where did they learn to fly?"

"Yeah. And to fly from?

"Mighty close to Kennebunkport."

"Yeah, that naval base the president left open."

"A roadside bomb. What is that?"

"Yeah. Why does it kill only one? What did the other guys do?"

"Duck."

"American people have a right to know; but foreigners know more."

"Every week the President says it's what we need to do."

"Wait a minute, wise guy. You wrote an essay over why we shouldn't always believe what we read. Why do you think differently about what someone says?"

"He's not someone; he's the President."

"Yeah, and he read a book."

"Better watch out, that someone may be listening."

"Oh, oh. There are spies amongst us! Everybody, empty your pockets, quick. Someone's gonna run us through a metal detector."

"Maybe there are bugs in the bulbs," offered Cinder.

Voices, background noises stopped. All students turned to look at Ms Smythe. She removed her gardening gloves and turned her body into a sitting position so she could look up at the bunch of seniors who had more at stake than planting bulbs. Their future. Their life.

"I will tell you this once. What you can do over what is troubling this nation and our soldiers is not ... I repeat ... not helped by tearing at the conscience of your friends. Emotion is a terrible thing to waste. Let it be a guide to what you think and your thinking will be as rotten as last year's bananas! Dried up rot! I know. I found one like that in my dorm.

"We all have a stake in this war. Whether it is an emotional one, a personal one, a rational or irrational one. A political or monetary one. We all are affected by it. War is a destructive thing. Just now I heard you try to destroy each other."

Cinder could not help herself. They were listening to her. She said the words no one had heard from her before. Not even Carla or Charrissa. Or Emily.

"Personally, what the war in Iraq means to me is that a soldier I love with all my heart MAY come home. I am not seasoned enough to know more than that. Knowing is the key, you see. It makes me feel weak and angry and selfish to not have the knowledge to surmount what I feel. And if I let you stand around arguing and worrying about it, we won't get these bulbs planted before it rains."

All young people could relate to rain. They burst into action.

It was Dannel who broke the suspended chatter. "Know what, Smythe? The last time we had to hustle to beat the rain was when you called us ghouls. Then you ate our sandwiches. Now you are calling upon us to hide something in the ground that might grow come Spring. Let's not underestimate this Smythe lady, guys. She's a piece of work."

"Wait 'til you season out our winter, Smythe, then you'll be seasoned enough." chided Ellen. "Come Thanksgiving? Be thankful you can afford good boots."

All bulb planters laughed as though they would burst.

Cinder lightened up, too. She felt close to these kids. Like them, she was in a fix over growing up. She did not feel she was there yet. She needed more work on that.

rACHEL

Ossie packed their gear while Rachel picked up the cabin. She tossed their bedded roses into the fireplace for good luck.

"It's early, yet," he said. "We could fly around a bit before heading home. Might even spot a bear snacking away on acorns."

"Bears and acorns? I asked Shute when he went rock hounding this weekend to get me some acorns. Fly told me once that acorns make good muffins."

"When did Fly tell you that?"

"He told me that when I was just a waitress. When I wasn't engaged to wed a wonderful man who happens to be a pilot and loves to teach me things, too!"

"Rachel, you are and never have been, just a waitress. Why, I think you are blossoming into one hell of a woman. I want to be right beside you all the way."

"Si, Ossie," she said into his shoulder, inside one of his gentle bear hugs. Her sisters were right. Ossie did not mind her scars. He did not love her anyway; however, he loved her all the way. "It's part of you," he said. "The you I love." Rachel never felt so much a woman. Or so beautiful. Walking. Flying. She desired to be with Ossie forever.

sHUTE

A long string of expletives erupted from Shute. Earlier he'd been fighting off deer flies from his balding head with his old fishing hat. Taking a long leak in a grove of pine trees. Feeling right and full of pride. Now he felt dust in his face as his jeep tore down the Golden Road. Headed for bear! How could he be so stupid! It was a fifty mile trek to get himself back to the supply station. So why was that trucker flagging him? The last thing on this driver's mind was a logging truck!

sALLY

Clumps of dirt upon their welcome rug continued up the stairs. Sally went directly to Dannel's door. It was ajar. She had expected to get after him for being so careless, instead she stopped. He was on the phone. His voice was shaky. Something was wrong. Sally was not sure what to do. She couldn't make a habit of listening in on Dannel's phone calls; but her mother's heart made her do just that.

"Well she wasn't there. Just tell me, Mrs. Crocker. What did Marley say, please? When she left. OK, what was she wearing? This is important, Mrs. Crocker. Will you call around? See if you can find her. No, I'm not trying to tell you how to be a parent!"

Sally took the phone from her son. "Mrs. Crocker? Jayne? Sally here. Dannel has a point. He's worried about Marley. I'm going to ask him why and call you back." Sally hung up the phone and turned to her son. "What's going on?"

Dannel did not hesitate. He gladly reached into his pocket and took out a crumpled piece of note paper. "Josh handed me this after we finished planting bulbs. You know, at school. I came home as fast as I could. I don't know what it means, Mom. I just want to find out where she is so I can talk to her about it.'

Seconds later, Sally called Jayne. Marley was not at home. Jayne did not know where she was. "Listen Jayne, I'm coming over. Marley sent Dannel a note. I think you should read it."

Sally turned to Dannel. "Call Fly. Read him this note and meet me in the car."

fLY

"Damn!" He'd just got off duty from a ten hour stretch. "Hello," he barked. "Dannel? What's going on? Sally all right?"

"I got this note, Fly. Josh said he'd had it since Friday. It's from that girl. You know, the one you caught me with last Wednesday."

"That slut?"

"She's no slut, Fly. Just gets freaked out over...over...."

"OK, Dannel. She smokes and drinks. Doesn't make her a slut."

"It does make her one messed up kid, Fly. And she blames me."

"Is this an official call, Dannel?" Fly groaned to hear that it was.

"Yes. I got this note today. It says:

'Dear Dannel, you were always my truest of true friends and I am sorry for all the trouble I've caused you. I want you to know that you've never let me down in any way. I wish it were enough. I'm not going to be a bother any more. I'm getting out. Going down river. One way. Please don't feel sorry for me. It's for the best. Love, Marley' "

"Two questions. One. When did she write that note? Two. She got a boat?"

"Yesterday. Josh gave it to me today. Right when we finished planting bulbs at the High School with Miss Smythe. Marley gave it to him sometime Friday. In school. I guess she could find a boat in the slip by Codger's Gap. We kids use them to reach the island. The water's high, now. No island. Just flowing water all the way to the dam."

Fly could hear the unseasoned sense of shaken vulnerability in his nephew's voice. Jesus, he thought. Kids have poor timing when it comes to facing reality. "I know about it. I'll get right on it, Dannel. Give me the stats."

"It's Marley Crocker. Mother, Jayne. Father, Ted. He's the High School Principal. Mom and I are going there now. Mom's idea." He gave the address and phone number, then added, "Mrs. Crocker said Marley stayed with friends last night and hasn't come home. She said her red silk shirt is missing. It's new. She got it to wear to the October Fest. Probably wouldn't need it. No one to take her."

Fly's mind began to work. Sleep or no, he thought fast. He was no good at figuring out what went on in the minds of teenagers. He had to stick to facts. Codger's Gap was ten miles above North Bend Dam. By the time Marley wrote that note, she may already have had a way to get there. His first call was to Amy. She stayed on top of things, that one.

"Sure, Fly. Shute went up to the St. John's River on Friday. He always spends two, three days picking river rocks and collecting geodes. I expect he'll be back sometime Sunday."

"Does he go alone?"

"Most times. Lest he finds a helper."

"Got a way to reach him?"

"Nope."

He knew she meant he could do it better.

"Amy, we got ourselves a possible runaway-suicide. Young girl. Marley Crocker. Wrote Dannel Harris a note on Friday. Seems to indicate she was going to Codger's Gap. Do you think she may have hitched with Shute? Her note said she was going down river. One way."

Fly wasn't surprised at the way Amy got right to the point. "Well, Fly. Vern's in that area. Probably in the air right now."

His second call was to Samantha. Luckily, she was on duty. "I'm checking out a possible suicide. Marley Crocker. High School Senior. Last seen Friday afternoon. Send out a call through dispatch. Wearing a red silk shirt. Long black hair. About a hundred pounds or so. Five feet, four or so. Got that? Alright, now patch me through to Paselli's plane. The piper."

vERN, *who is Rachel's Ossie*

He was right. This woman was bursting out right before his eyes. Was it love that made him see her this way? Or was it love that made her look that way? Either way, he loved the excitement in her as she looked at the view below them. And at him. His Rachel. Made him feel like a crazy college kid. It took him off course when his radio cracked from Fly. Fly wasn't one of his favorite people.

"This better be good, Fly. I'm on a tight schedule."

Rachel laughed beside him. Then she gasped at Fly's response.

"There's a runaway, possible suicide," cracked the radio. "Teenage girl. Red shirt. Marley Crocker. May have hitched a ride last night. She might be fetching a boat from Codger's Gap. Can you scout it out?"

"There are no boats on the river near there, Fly. We just passed it. What time frame we talking here? We're flying North toward the border. Toward St. John's River."

fLY

Fly sat in Crocker's driveway and called Samantha once more. "How you going with that missing person? I think you better contact truckers. See who she asked for rides and where she wanted to go. North is only one direction. First, though, get in touch with the Ranger Station. Have them try to find Shute on St. John's river, near St. John's Bay. Paselli's flying up there. He'll call in if he spots anything. Let me know what you hear. I'm at Crocker's."

Once inside the Crocker's tidy two story home, Fly noted Mr. Crocker was watching the game. His wife sat stiffly at her kitchen table. She was holding a cup of tea with the bag still in it. Marley's note was next to her right hand. Sally and Dannel sat there, too. Fly ignored Crocker and sat beside Dannel at the table. He cupped his hand on his nephew's shoulder. "I got two things. Marley was seen at Murphy's Friday afternoon asking truckers for rides. She may have hitched a ride from one of them or from Shute. He was heading up to St. John's to do some rock picking. The second thing is Paselli just flew over by Codger's Gap. He didn't see any boats on the river. He's scouting around though."

Jayne Crocker turned her head ever so slowly toward Fly. Her eyes were dark. He felt she would lash out at him for bringing Paselli into it. So he spoke fast. "We've got dispatches going out. To truckers, radio, all police, game wardens, and to the nearest Ranger Station where Shute may be."

"Marley doesn't have an interest in rocks, or Grover Shute."

Fly nodded, asked Dannel. "What did you find out from Josh?"

Dannel answered. "Josh's on his way over. Wants to talk to you. I think he's afraid you're going to arrest him. For withholding evidence."

Jayne Crocker stood up, then. "Well, I guess if we're going to keep having quests, I'll make some sandwiches."

eLLEN

Out of respect for her mother, Ellen removed her soiled shoes and socks. She could hear the vacuum working in the back bedroom. In a minute she'd go inside to check on Mrs. Young. For now she sat alone on the steps and thought about Smythe. What would it really take, she wondered, to be seasoned enough? Mrs. Young came out and sat beside her. Handed her a soda. Ellen smiled. It was diet. Caffeine free.

"I'm so sorry I didn't pick you up. I wanted to. I left myself a note; but, you see, I fell asleep." Mrs. Young put her hands on her knees and sighed.

Seconds later, Ellen's mother was rushing out to Mrs. Young and Ellen was saying, "Please send an ambulance to thirty-one Bartell Street. Take the third left turn after the High School. It's Frieda Young. She's white as a ghost. She just came home from the hospital, you know. For cancer. Call back if there's a problem. This is Ellen."

Ellen called another number. "Billy? This is Ellen. I want you to go to the soccer game right now and find Mr. Young and the twins. Tell Mr. Young his wife is sick. I've called the ambulance. Tell Mr. Young to bring the twins home."

It had been less than five minutes. Ellen's mother had wrapped a soft blanket around Mrs. Young and was holding onto her as best she could. Ellen stood calmly in the doorway to watch for the ambulance, listening to the two women talk.

"For a strong woman, Mrs. Young, you sure have slender shoulders."

"Thank you, Amy."

kEVIN

"See Billy run," said Kade.

"Run, Billy, run," said Dean.

Kevin looked to where his boys were waving. Sure enough. Billy Trent was running! Billy was sweet on Ruby and had came around most everyday quite close to supper time. Frieda insisted that everyone sit down to eat together. Even Billy. A much more kempt Billy than how he looked running pel mel toward where Kevin and the twins were sitting. No hat and moving without his crutches. So Kevin knew something was wrong. It was the first time Kevin felt respect for the man.

fRIEDA

Something was wrong. Frieda knew. Amy? No. Ruby. Thank you, Ruby. She was afraid. She wanted Amy. White coats. Latex covered hands. Telling her to breathe. Sirens. Oh, such bumpy roads. No time to say any last goodbyes. How could she talk anyway? So much noise. Was she there yet? "Is it soup yet?" She wanted to ask. She guessed she'd have to wait. Wait for Kevin. Wait for her mother. Kade and Dean. Dean and Kade. Her twins. Voices said for her to relax. What could they mean? And so, there came a poem.

> *Oh, what a noise was made, Kade.*
> *Playing me a siren, Dean.*

Then everything around Frieda dimmed.

aMY

Amy heard the ambulance charging along Bartell and closed the large wooden door to the Anchorage. "Go home," she told everyone. "Love your family. It's Frieda. I'll call you when I hear something."

vICTORIA

Mrs. Victoria Abbott Harrington Coumbs had been sleeping. Else she would have answered the phone right away. It probably didn't matter, except Kevin's impatience was hard to forgive over what he had to tell her. Over what her daughter confessed he'd been doing to his family for the last three years. "Pick up, Mother! It's Frieda. She's on the way to the hospital. I'm on my way to pick you up. Please be ready."

Victoria did not let herself fault him. She found her jacket and shoes. Her hat and gloves. She called her daughter's number. Ellen answered. Such a fine young lady, that Ellen.

"Kevin ... Mr. Young ... is on his way. Don't worry. Dean and Kade are safe with Mumma and me. Kade and Dean are here, safe. Mrs. Young got faint. I called the ambulance. Mumma says it's the medicine that made her sick. Mumma said she had green tea and lay down for a nap around nine. Ate half a tuna sandwich at noon. Said she was tired and slept until I got home. She did not know my mother."

Victoria gave some comfort to her son in law. "Thank you, Kevin, for loving my wonderful daughter." She could say no more. She needed strength for Frieda now.

fLY

"So, was it three o'clock, or ten? Seems a young fella like you could remember details better'n that." Fly sat back in his chair and stared incredulously at this stubborn young man. "When did you get that note? Why didn't you give it to Dannel right away? Let's not beat around here, boy. A girl's missing. You know something I don't. Did you see her write that note? Is that it? She tell you to wait?"

"It's OK, Josh. Fly doesn't have much patience. I get the picture. Marly was always writing notes. She ever write you any, Josh? A please, please, please help me note? A love note? I always figured I wasn't the only one that got them. Don't tell me you were jealous?"

"Of you? No way." As he spoke, Josh looked from Dannel, to Fly, to Mrs. Crocker. Only Mrs. Crocker did not look at him. "She gave it me about three o'clock, Officer Fly. 'This is important', she said. 'Please give it to Darnnel.' I mean, she said it straight out. Like she wrote notes to Dannel everyday."

"Not everyday."

"First I knew. It took me back a bit. Made me nervous to be the middle guy. I thought it was a love note. I didn't see any hurry to give it to him. I read it about ten o'clock today. I got it right to Dannel after I read it. If I hadn't of read it, you never would have gotten it, Dannel."

"I owe you one, Josh. You done good. Good as anyone."

"School was over by then, Josh?" Fly wanted facts.

"Yeah. We had an assembly. Smoke Out or something. I spent most of it in the bathroom. Just hanging out. Marley asked me to meet her after school. I was getting ready. I was hoping she knew of a party to go to. I would've taken her. Turns out all she wanted was a favor. Over a note. Last I saw of her was her walking over toward Main Street. Past the barber shop. She may have gone to Murphy's. She knows some truckers that pull in there. She gets dope off 'em. 'S'nother reason I gots angry. Marly always has extra money. I guessed she wasn't sharing."

Both Darnel and Mrs. Crocker gasped.

Sally spoke first. "You ever give her money, Dannel?

Mrs. Crocker sighed heavily.

Josh said, "Sorry, Mrs. Crocker. I did sometimes. I thought I was helping."

"Me, too, Josh. Me, too. Lots times." Dannel's words came harder than Josh's.

"And you, Jayne? Did you give her money?" Sally's voice was calm, quiet.

Mrs. Crocker huffed and pushed her hands against the table. "I always keep money in my purse. I lose track sometimes. It goes quite fast. I never asked Marly about it."

"Why?" asked Fly.

"Well, Teddy, you know. He comes by sometimes. I guessed he needed money."

Fly knew about Teddy. Crocker's errant son. Been gone mostly a year. Fly did not bother to talk to Crocker. "About how much in the last couple of weeks?"

"Maybe a hundred. Maybe more." The implication was brimming Mrs. Crocker over with tears.

"Sally," gestured Fly.

Sally went to her friend. They left the room.

"Don't look at me, Fly," protested Dannel. "I never took from my mother's purse. I have a job, remember? Marly always got cozy around payday."

"She-it!" Josh cocked an anxious eye in Crocker's direction. He didn't need to worry. The old man was snoring.

~6~

.....!Details, directions, discussions, decisions! Why Billy?!

vERN, *who is Rachel's Ossie*

Just short of St. John's River Crossing, Vern saw Shute. A trucker had flagged him down. Two figures were standing in front of Shute's jeep. One of them turned to wave at his plane.

Rachel said she knew them.

Vern reached for his radio.

Kevin

Kevin had thought the worst. They'd been told to watch for setbacks. Amy had come to wait with him and Frieda's mother. They seemed to find it hard to have a look at him. It wasn't that he didn't deserve their reserved way of treating him. But now, he jumped with relief at Doctor Eiser's reassurance.

"It was a close call. Frieda blacked out in the ambulance. She was dehydrated. We can't overlook those little signs. It's serious. We've got an IV started. We need to keep her until her blood count improves and we have the dehydration under control. You've got quite a crew to watch out over her, I hear. That's good. But you should watch her. Don't let her overextend. Make sure she drinks enough liquids. She'll be fine if she takes it slow. The crisis is over. She can continue her therapy. Be home in a few days. "

Kevin understood he could no longer take Frieda for granted. He motioned for Victoria to go first to visit Frieda. Amy went with her. Kevin welcomed the reprieve from Victoria's sidelong glances.

Doctor Eiser asked, "How are you doing, Kevin?"

He hadn't expected the question. Didn't know how to respond.

"I know this is hard on you, Kevin. You should know this, too. Don't be hard on yourself. If you need me for anything, I can be there for you. Happy to help. Everyone done good. Frieda, too. You got a tiger there, for sure."

Victoria was smiling at him. Kevin hugged her before stumbling down the hall to see his wife. He was careful to thank Amy for coming. He could feel the tension ebbing from his groin. Hear the blood relax in his brain. I'm worth having Frieda for a wife, he thought. This is not a second chance. This is part of what to expect. Uncertain things happen to a family.

Frieda was propped up on the bed in a mass of pillows.

"The sports report is: Team Frieda has won again. What's this about sliding down hill? I thought you were going to climb up."

Frieda laughed softly. He had expected as much. "Oh, you," she cooed. "Stop looking at me as though I'm an angel."

Kevin dead panned her into another laugh. "You mean it's a disguise?" And then he cried upon her stomach. "It's OK to show off. Dr. Eiser said so."

mARLEY

Marley's back hurt. She shivered from the cold and could not feel her legs. Luckily, she got inside the tent ... how, she could not remember ... and it was saving her from the mosquitoes.

She wasn't sure how far off the road she was. It had been dark when she fell. When the tent slipped. And the pain. Tearing and banging and bending and pulling her body. Always there each time she regained consciousness. Making her terrified. Terrified they would not find her. Terrified they would find her not OK. Or not find her at all.

fLY

Jayne Crocker handed him the phone. No expression showed on her face. He supposed it was Samantha. "Yes." Fly listened. "Yes. Send it out right away." Fly stood up and grabbed for his coat. "Work's done here," he told the women. "You boys can come with me, now. Sally, stay here. Some good news. We're going to start a land search near the Trading Post. There's no boat. I'll call as soon as I have something to report."

sHUTE

"Yeah, I seen her. Annoying little pismire. Always wanting something. Hanging around Murphy's and down by the tracks. Hitchhiking. She mad at me for ditching her? Climbed into my jeep, she did. I never even noticed her until I got to post. When I found her all curled up in the back of my jeep, I yanked her out and made her go inside. Farley will tell you that. Made her call her mother. 'Come get me!' You know, wasn't my responsibility to cart her home after the way she hid out like that. Well, when I got the gear I wanted, she was no where 'round. 'Good!' I said. I thought Farley'd hold on to her. I stopped to take a piss just short of my camping place. That's when I noticed the missing beer. And my missing tent. Had that old thing for years and just like that. Gone. I drank a couple beers and fumed all night over it. This morning, I come to a change of mind over Marley. If she had my tent, then she must be off somewhere's around the post. I set out to find her. Yeah, I know that was selfish of me. Any straight thinking man would of taken her straight home. Thing is, I'd been drinking. Better that she got her mother. Let me get back to what I was doing."

Not even Shute appreciated his compulsive flow of words. Yet he was annoyed that the trucker who stopped him was waving at a plane.

jAYNE cROCKER

Mrs. Jayne Crocker wiped the stray hairs from her forehead. "I don't feel anything about Marley, Sally. Not deep down. Just pains in my neck and my eyebrows. I'm going to have one of my headaches. I've got to lie down. First, I better drink something. It'll help me wake up."

Mrs. Crocker drank some orange juice to help her swallow two pills. She ate three soda crackers. She went to the bathroom. Sally covered her on her bed. Mrs. Crocker covered her eyes with a wet washcloth. A dark one to keep out the light. She did some slow, deep breathing. About five times. Then the migraine hit and she hoped she could hold down the orange juice long enough to fall asleep.

bILLY

When the word got out about a search for Marley, Billy hurried down to the firehouse. People were milling around waiting for instructions. From what he could gather, the best place for a search point was at the Trading Post. "It's got a radio, telephones, food, repellent, batteries. You can set up there and start the search parties."

Billy had been in charge of searches before his own lost-in-the-woods episode. Now he wanted to be again. But not on the mountain.

Fly said he was glad to see Billy. He told him what he knew from Shute. "I'm full up and ready to meet up with searchers at the Trading Post. I got extra blankets, mosquito netting, coffee pots, toilet paper, cups, rain gear, first aid, and water in the van. I think people should bring flashlights and sleeping gear, if they have it. Dress warm. Wear boots. If you can handle things from here, Billy, I'll feel better. Get someone to drive me. I need some sleep. Me and the two boys here are taking the van. We're following the Rescue Truck. Oh, the guy in charge up there is Arnold. Here's the call code."

"Yep." Billy took over right away. Posted the supplies list on the front door. Asked people to sign up with their home phone numbers and as to how they were going and what they had. Got a driver for Fly. Remembered to send a bull horn with the van. Within minutes, people were car pooling and on their way. Other officials were on the way. Game Wardens, too. Billy found out who they were from Samantha. She gave him the names of truckers and the information she had from Vern.

When the reporters arrived, it was Billy who met them. Billy who told them Marly was lost in the woods. "She went on a trip up North and got separated from her party. There's a united search beginning right now. We've got an area pinpointed between St. John's Bay and the Trading Post at the beginning of The Golden Road. All I can personally say is it rained last night. She probably stayed put. That will help the search." Billy did not answer any more questions. He knew it wouldn't help. Reporters would know what they needed to know soon enough. Especially, the ones who opted to go to the search point by the Trading Post.

cINDER

She knew Billy. She'd met him at Young's. "Hi," she said kindly, thinking he had come to watch. "What's the news? Who's got the word? How can we help?"

"Ah, Miss Cinder Smythe," answered Billy in his warm voice. "We've got things underway and going strong. What I'd like for you to do is take charge of this list thing. You know, we don't want to lose anyone else up there. Gotta get it to the search point."

Cinder felt awed by his directions. This was a new Billy. Not the unassuming one who sat at Frieda's kitchen table while Ruby worked around him. Not the one in grubby overalls who quietly suggested she not buy the car she found because it was a clunker looking for a new timing belt, new paint, new tires, and exhaust system. She had listened to him then; she took the clipboard from him now. "Shucks, Billy. Just what I always wanted. Attendance chart."

"Well, so's you know, you asked," chuckled Billy, whose bedroom eyes made it important to listen. "Fax number for The Trading Post, in the phone book. Going to Arnold. Calling code. Top of the list."

"Well, I'll do my best, Billy. The penmanship is a real challenge!"

"Yeah. Send it anyway. You can follow up with corrections later. Ask the natives, if you can get their attention. Oh, on your cover letter, you can ask for them to double check. Case someone doesn't show." He grinned. "You know, like a field trip."

"Right," agreed Cinder. She had underestimated Billy. Ouch, she thought. And him the boss! Cinder sent her fax before ascending the handful of 'natives' to help her with the names on her clipboard. Some she had not come across before. If not for the trauma, it could be fun.

vERN, *who is Rachel's Ossie*

They buzzed low over The Golden Road. South, then North again. Sighting birds and moose. Rachel spotted it first. The little clearing where moss that was not moss could be seen just to the outer edge.

"That looks like Spanish moss. Hugging a tree. On the ground, too. Is that what it is? They have lots of that moss in At Lanta. I didn't know it grew in Maine."

"Lichen. We have a fair amount of that. On rocks and trees. Moose like it."

"Looks odd to me," tsked Rachel. Like she had so much to learn.

"Odd? It's the odds we are looking for, right?"

Excitement flowed from Rachel as Vern began turning the plane for another look at what she saw. This time he flew low. "There it is. I see it! It's a shelter place, Ossie. I think it is a tent. A flat tent. Do you think someone was there? It looks old."

Seconds later, Rachel saw movement. "Some bears! I see bears!"

Vern got on the radio and called it in to the Ranger Station. After giving the coordinates, he mentioned the broken pine tree and the pile of logs that once fell off a logging truck. Lastly, he mentioned the bears. He called Samantha to report these same details. "Fuel's getting low. We gotta turn back. Call you when we get there."

aMY

"Hello," said Amy. She hoped it was Vern. It wasn't.

"Hello, Amy. This is Rachel. I loved those red roses. Muchos gracias! Vern wants to tell you what happened."

In the pause between Rachel's voice, before Vern took the phone, Amy felt Vern's whole life flash before her eyes. Rachel? Of course, Rachel! Not to be melodramatic, she asked, "Was it you, or the roses?"

Amy let Vern know how delighted the news made her feel before she asked about Shute. His laugh was still in her ears when she hung up.

mARLEY

The flies were buzzing louder this time. Marley tried to breathe slowly so as not to attract them with her scent. She waited for them to crush her head. Waited for them to puncture her arms and legs. She must have been sick. She could feel the vomit that stuck to her chin and arm. Her head throbbed! Was this the pain her mother had? Before she passed out again, before the noise stopped in her brain, she thought her mother was rocking her. She lay quiet so as not to frighten her away.

cINDER

"It's amazing, isn't it Miss Smythe? People stopping what they are doing to brave the Northern woods in late fall to search for someone they might not even know or care about in ordinary circumstances? I hope they ain't disappointed," said Billy in his slow, serious voice. He handed Cinder a cup of coffee, made to her unique liking: half coffee, half milk. Cinder studied his rather bedroomy eyes ... as in the college phrase used by she, Carla, and Charissa toward older, seasoned and sexually conducive men ... in sharp contrast to the situation at hand. She blushed; but he had not noticed. He had already spun around upon his crutches to make way toward the crowd of people coming through the firehouse doorway. Among them were Amy, Vern Paselli, and Rachel from Murphy's.

Billy and Vern moved aside together in deep conversation.

Cinder went to join Amy and Rachel. "Did you bring good news? You sure look especially well. Both of you.

Before congratulating Rachel on her engagement, Cinder took a long sip of coffee.

sHUTE

By the time Shute made it to the post, it was crawling with men and women in green clothing. Six or seven of them. They stood around looking at charts. Scratching their heads. Shute hit the ground running. "Where's Arnold?"

A tall, skinny man whom Shute did not know pointed to a heavy set man leaning against a shiny green pickup. As Shute approached, the man turned belligerent on him.

"What the hell you think you're doing, dropping a young girl off in the woods to fend for herself? You better have something decent to say to me right now, mister, or you can just pack yourself out of my face."

"What the hell you doin' standing around, A?" Shute's muscular thin body showed no backing down. "Vern as much as told you where she was. Came over the squawk box. Leave the rest of that shit be, A. I know the spot. It's in the opposite direction from where I was headed. Know something, Arnold? You can't get there from here less'n you cross that chasm below the loop. Logging truck took a flip there when the tires blew out three years back. Gonna need ropes to get a stretcher down there. You got any walkies? Get the medicals and let's go."

Arnold let his hackles show. "We're going to stay organized, Shute. There are people on the way. You park your ass...."

Shute backed away. Saluted Arnold. Did an about face. Walked over to the skinny guy and began to bark orders. "Arnold wants you people to mark your maps. Right here. See? The Loop. This is where we need to search. You gotta set up right about here. I need three able bodied people to come with me. We're going down the chasm. We need water, ropes, walkies, and medicals. My jeep's over here. It'll get us close. Take an hour to reach her. Send the crews just as soon as Arnold can get them organized. Turn here, see? On the map. Come on. Move."

There was a flurry of activity while Shute barked orders. Before Arnold had any idea of what was happening, Shute's jeep was flying down the Golden Road toward the old narrow logging road used once before to rescue a trucker and what was left of his logging truck. Shute's mind was set. He was after his tent. And she better be with it!

Shute stopped just before the loop, before the chasm. Two truckers and a game warden were with him. He had one more direction. "We need a marker for the turn off. I got some white paint in the back. Anything else you can find that will work? Go for it."

fLY

"Arnold's on the horn."

Fly nodded. It was the third contact from him. Fly told him straight out the last time to not call him again unless he had something.

Of course he had something. "It's something about Shute." Fly had to take it.

"This better be good. I'm on a half hour of sleep in twenty."

"We got a wild card up here. Name of Shute. The one who lost the girl in the first place. Took three good men and headed to the loop. Turned on a side road. Said he'd mark it. It's about twenty miles from the loop. Closest way in to where Paselli's plane spotted the tent. I've got another crew on the way. They'll be waiting for you on the Loop. According to Billy, Shute knows what he's doing."

"Right," responded Fly, ending the conversation.

Spaulding shook his head.

"What's that, Spaulding? You on to Shute, too?"

"Well no, Fly. I'm on to Arnold."

"Just drive, Spaulding. Let me sleep."

Seconds later, Fly was on the horn to Billy about Shute.

sHUTE

Shute found himself in pretty good company. Clyde Omer and Shawn Upton drove diesel trucks. Each was surprised to learn that the other took up jogging for their health between long hauls. Pearl Hendrickson had been a paramedic with rescue in Lewiston before becoming a Game Warden. She was an avid outdoorswoman and was a pretty good photographer. Shute told them he took regular trips up into the mountains for rocks. "I got my own gem shop; but I haul dirt 'n gravel to make a living."

The four of them made short work of marking the beginning of the tote road. They even left a poster of who they were and what time they turned off. Pearl worked on another such marker for the end of the tote road. A friendly group, not much talk came from them. All were worried about the thickening dark clouds coming from the West.

mARLEY

The blackflies were back. Making funny sounds. Bloodthirsty bastards. Coming at her like that. There must be thousands and thousands of them. Hovering over her. Why was help taking so long? Was there a game being played on her? Dannel? She closed her eyes. In the dark, only her Mother could find her. But her Mother growled and snorted at her. "I'm not a boogey man, Marley. Wake up and see for yourself." So Marley opened her eyes and yelled. Over and over. It seemed to be working. Dark shadows stopped coming at her. Then there were more of them. Charging her cover. Calling her name. Making hums that sounded like "God". Marley's moans gurgled in her throat. When they were upon her at last, she gave in to them. To the void of wanting her mother. To wanting to run and run and run. To know what to do. About the darkness.

sHUTE

Sweat penetrated through Shute's outer clothing. He mopped his red hanky profusely under his hat and along his shoulders. The deerflies were hovering, waiting for the barrier of fly dope to weaken. Past noon. Shute and his trio hadn't finished the downhill part of their trek. Pearl's insistence on laying a retraceable path made sense to Shute, but the extra time and extra work were taking their toll.

"OK. Rest. Grab a drink. Five minutes."

No one argued. In fact, all hit the ground at once and sighed in unison. When they did, a yelling sound chilled any talk amongst them. Shute sprang to his feet. "Bear!" He was aware that the others were following him closely. And that he and his trio were closer to The Loop than he had anticipated. "I'm coming, you bastards!"

Pearl clipped by Shute in her strong stride. "What do you think you'll do, Shute, if there is a bear? Tackle it with your bare hands?"

"No," shouted Shute. "We're making more noise than a pack of elephants. Ain't no bear gonna stick around and wait for us!"

They moved together in long strides. Sliding over rocks and slipping around fallen trees. Calling out to Marley. Then they found it. The scraped earth and broken braches. Still evident from the old log spill. This was to be Shute's reference point. Instead, as Vern's message should have alerted him, it was the site of recent damage. Something or someone had left fresh marks and broken branches right on down to the bottom of the chasm. Shute looked up to where he could see the loop's railing above him. The others did, too. Shute was thinking it was too far to fall and live.

"God," said Shute. "It's awful high up."

Shawn took up his radio to call it in.

"Tell Rescue to look for your marker, Shawn. Tell them to start lowering ropes and a stretcher ASAP. Then stay there for our signal!"

Pearl led the others downward to the clearing. Her throaty voice boomed out over the tree tops. "We're coming, Marley. Wait for us, Marley. Can you hear us, Marley? Marley? Do you hear us, Marley?"

The scene they came upon was not the one Shute had hoped for.

"Not good," surmised a huffing and puffing Clyde.

"Nope," grunted Shute.

The bear had pawed around the tent. There was blood where it had been. A lot of blood. Pearl got down to touch it. "It's wet," she said.

"God," breathed Shute between his teeth. He reached for his knife. He'd have to cut her out of the tent.

Clyde held out his hand. "She's under the flap, Shute. What's left of her. Oh, God!"

Pearl threw off her back pack. "This is a rescue, fellas," she reminded the men. "We rescue. Do what we can. Leave the rest up to the licensed people. Now, set up the flares and open that flap. Marley? Marley, can you hear me? Goddamn it, Marley, speak!"

It was Shute's role to follow the leader. He set up flags and flares while Clyde opened the flap. Shute signaled Shawn to let him know they had contact. Shute almost had a heart attack when Pearl's voice rang out, loud and clear. Loud enough for Shawn to hear.

"I got a pulse!"

The rain, that they knew would come, fell heavily upon them.

aRNOLD

"Yeah, I got something! Heard from Shawn. They found where she fell. They can see the tent. Get to the Loop and slow down. Look down the South grade for Shawn's yellow flag. Word is to have Rescue ready with a stretcher to lower down to Shawn. He says it's quite a drop. Did you get that?"

"Got it? Best news of the day!"

"No. The best news is they heard her yell."

The worst news is he almost blew it. His first rescue detail and he almost killed the messenger! If that girl gets pulled out alive, Arnold'd stake that good for nothing Shute to a year's worth of park passes! Or maybe a new tent!

fRIEDA

There was a good chance she might make it to her poetry book signing after all. She wanted to tell Amy she had offered the bear another helping and it had worked. Frieda asked for a pad and pencil. She wanted to write a poem. A poem about getting a hold on life again.

bILLY

Fly's call came right after Arnold's. Billy had to quiet the cheering so he could hear. "No one's told her, Fly."

"Well, get the word over there. Can't leave Sally on hold."

Fly was right. This was the hardest part of any search and rescue. Hearing good news, waiting for the rest of the story, and relaying the news to the parents who were waiting for word at home. The small area in the firehouse was so quiet, Billy could hear the water dripping on the outside faucet. Until he asked for volunteers! He sent Phil Pelletier, and Beatrice

Rye right away. He sent Vern Paselli, too, because he knew details first hand. Phil and Beatrice were neighbors and friends of the Crocker's. Others, because it could be a long vigil, signed up with Cinder as a change of guard or as a casserole brigade.

"We also need food," pronounced Billy. "Bagels and coffee?"

jAYNE cROCKER

Ted answered the door and shook Vern's hand. Jayne Crocker did not hear what they said. It sounded like good news. From her livingroom chair, Jayne saw Phil and Bea place food containers from Murphy's on her table.

Sally patted her hand. "They have food, Jayne. I guess they plan to stay."

Sally's overture of genuine feeling gave Jayne courage. "I don't want to lose Marley, Sally. Does Vern know where she is? Oh, please, bring her home." Jayne pulled the pillow she was hugging up to her face and smothered her words. Ted sat down beside her. Bea and Phil came and hugged her, then went with Sally to fix plates of food.

It was left up to Vern to give the news. All eyes except Jayne's looked up to him. "We know this," he began. "A foursome led by Shute went into the woods. It took them over an hour to make their way to the crash site below The Loop. That's where Marley fell. The good news is, she was alive and breathing when they found her further down in the chasm. The bad news is, she has a lot of cuts and lost a lot of blood from her injuries. They're giving her first aid now. I guess she was holding onto a tent when she fell. That's where they found her. Under the tent. She's hurt, weak, and ... and .... I hate to be the one to tell you this. She may have been soused. Probably why she didn't try to stop herself from rolling so far. Probably helped her survive the fall. The last word was, she has a pulse, she has passed out, and it's raining."

"The Loop?" Jayne's face left her pillow. "That's bear country, Vern. How could you think this news would make me feel better?"

"Shucks, MS Jayne. She'sfound. 'Sall I know."

Jayne stood then, and took Vern's hand. "I know you're responsible for that. I am so glad you were up in that plane. I am just afraid of the worst. Why don't we eat?" She turned to Mr. Crocker. He had been showing a great deal of concern over Marley's disappearance. Only good could come from Marley's being found. Being home again. She was sure of it. "Come join us, Ted. We can relax better on a full stomach. It will make the waiting easier."

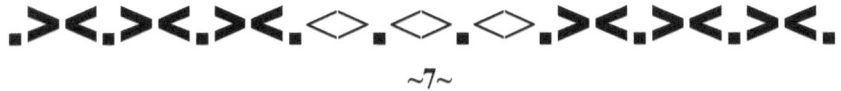

!AND *what effect DOES the search on the mountain have on others?!*

.,.><.><.◇.◇.◇.><.><.,..

eLLEN

Although Ellen often said Marley was an accident looking for a place to happen, she must not have believed it. When Billy told of the tragic state in which Marley was found, Ellen was as horrified as any of the young people standing helplessly around the fire station.

"I want you to go home now," Billy told them authoritatively. "Come back on a full stomach. If you want to hang out here, it's OK; but come with your own supplies. Nothing I would be upset about."

Mr. Young stopped his Subaru Forrester to pick up Ellen. First he told her Frieda was going to be OK. Then he thanked her for acting so quickly. "You saved her life, Ellen. You're our heroine! Now, what are you doing out here in the rain?"

Ellen's façade broke. "You know, Mr. Young, I ain't brave at all. Or too awful smart. I act on impulse. Mrs. Young saved herself, you know. When she came outside with a diet coke. I don't drink diet coke. Neither does she. You do. Anyone would've noticed that.

"I wish we could've noticed Marley more, so she didn't have to run away. You know, Marley Crocker, everyone's bitching post? They found her. She fell off the Loop. Tent and all. Doesn't it make you want to take back every foul thought you ever gave toward her, Mr. Young? Don't you just want to run all the way to The Loop and say, 'Marley, don't give up. I care. I really do!' Don'tcha?"

They were in the driveway by now. Mr. Young gripped the wheel. "Let me sink this in, Ellen. Marley ran away with a tent and fell off a loop? What am I missing here?"

Ellen laughed. It felt good to laugh. It took her five minutes to tell Mr. Young what really happened. She told him as far as she knew, Marley was seriously hurt, but alive.

Mr. Young told her she was right to think what she must be thinking; except he warned her that it is easier to see things sometimes in hindsight. Like it or not. "We can't always be ready, Ellen. I wasn't ready about Frieda's cancer. I wasn't ready to stop drinking. Marley wasn't ready for whatever was bothering her. In hindsight, I guess she was bothered by it for a long time. I'm sorry. All we can do now is hope. And hope it is enough."

By the time they went inside, Ellen's tears had dried; she allowed herself to listen quietly as Mr. Young told her mother and Sammy about Frieda. He in turn listened quietly as she told them about Marley. Something was clicking in her heart. She could hardly bear the emotions that set upon her. They made her feel separate and alone. In spite of her mother's gushing hug.

rUBY

Her daughter was no heroine. She was being herself. Ruby knew. She had seen her do things. Kind and deliberate things. Sometimes without thinking. Other times she would turn away. It was not about growing up. It was about survival. Her daughter ... no matter how much love Ruby gave her ... needed to understand that for herself. And so, Ruby tried to help her.

"Ellen, please listen to me for a bit. I really don't know what it is I need to say to you about Marley. Just let me try. Some kids your age just feel vulnerable. They don't know about survival. You do know. I am proud for your courage. So I ask, if you weed your neighbor's garden and the weeds grow back, what does that say to you?'

Ellen said, "I know this one. There are more weeds to hoe than there are hoes."

"I just want to let you off the hook, Ellen. Remember the story Stone Soup? Everyone put something into a pot and thought their wonderful meal came from nothing? Life is like that, you know. Always needing a little work. One stone, one weed at a time."

Ellen kissed Ruby's cheek. Slid down upon soft pillows on the couch and sighed.

It was enough for Ruby to know that whether or not Ellen understood what she meant, at least this sensitive child, her chosen daughter, would rest quietly for now.

dANNEL

As soon as Spaulding pulled the white van in behind Arnold's pickup, Dannel and Josh could see Rescue already had the stretcher out of the truck and were attaching the ropes. Both boys wanted to jump out and help. Fly, however, told them to put on rain gear and stay out of the way. "You'll be needed soon enough. Stay ready."

Josh looked down into the chasm with him, the long way down to where Marley had fallen. At the man standing by the yellow flag. At the tiny people below them who seemed to be doing some kind of dance. He hugged at his arms helplessly.

"Josh," said Dannel in his smallest of small voices, "I'm sorry. I don't know what to say. She's gotta be bad off. Real bad off."

"I feel sick," said Josh. Then he acted upon what he said.

The rain had slowed them; but other vehicles came with volunteers. Sounds and voices carried clearly in the rain. People couldn't hear themselves talk. Arnold got on the horn and asked for quiet. "We need to communicate on the work ahead, folks. Everyone stay focused. Nobody, I mean nobody gives an interview to the press before clearing it with me. Get the facts. And be kind to the rest of us."

The press? Dannel saw them. A news camera was filming the Rescue team. Because of the exposure they might put upon Marley, he wanted to ask them to leave, but what could he do? He looked again down the chasm. At how it was washed in rain. At the men guiding the stretcher downward. At men sliding down the water soaked ropes. Mud squished out as their feet hit the ground. The activity far below, in the small clearing, was where his heart lay. He could hear it thumping. He wanted to let it pump for Marley. Give her strength. He wanted to take back what he had said to her. He wanted her to be OK. Knew she wasn't. Knew she was in pain! Dannel felt a tearing in his stomach and cried out, "Josh, I want to get down there."

Josh put his hand upon Dannel's shoulder. "When she's in the stretcher and gets close to the yellow flag, ask Arnold. If she's conscious. Then, maybe."

Dannel didn't wait. He put on gloves and belt and lowered himself down the rope. He may be big, but he was strong. He was rope climbing champion in his gym class. Though that wasn't the same as this, Dannel felt confident that he could make it to Marley. That he could help her. He did not hear the yells from the men above. He only wanted to find Shute and tell him he done good. And then, his rope ran out.

pEARL

The girl seemed lifeless. Clyde had opened the flap as far back as he could so they could work on her. Pearl placed the oxygen valve over Marley's mouth and pumped three times. Clyde gave Marley three pushes on her chest. They tried again in spite of the rain.

Pearl was the first to beg off. To say it wasn't working. "Damn it, Marley," she cried at the girl. "You gonna quit just like that? Then why did you yell? Answer me, you little prick. You think I'm out here for my health? You called me here and all you do is lay there like a sack of potatoes? I have six more puffs to shove down your windpipe. I want you to get ready to exhale! On the count of five."

There was no need for Pearl to count.

sHAWN

Shawn, standing between the Loop and the rescue going on below him, let the cold rain replace the uncomfortable itching sweat across his aching body. He thought he had three priorities. He had taken the flu shot. His wife made him do it. He felt if worse came to worse his efforts here could only lead to a cold and sore muscles. Until others came down to help him, he was responsible for his radio and passing on information. As long as there was no lightning, he saw no reason but for the rescue to go smoothly. No danger to himself. Yelling from above got him to look up just as a large bundle came down at him. It seemed to have come off the rope. This was the first blunder of the day, he thought. Later he would tell his story this way. "Came right at me. I ran right under it. Thought it was blankets. Never occurred to me, it was Dannel Harris. Dammed near smacked my life out of me. We slammed together just like this." Shawn smacked the palms of his hands together and turned them sideways toward his shoulder and pulled them downward.

"The worse thing about it, was the way he yelled into my ear. Or maybe it was the weight of him pushing me into the mud. 'Twas the mud that saved me from being crushed like a pancake. Damnest thing ever happened to me. No football tackle ever made could top that'n! Know what I told him? I told him if he ever yelled at me like that again, I'd take that tongue of his out and feed it to the coyotes!" Shawn's faced beamed. "He looked like he believed me, too. Damn right, I meant it!"

mARLEY

Marley was not alone anymore. Someone was hitting her in the chest and face. Again and again. Someone in an angry voice was threatening her. Then the rain splashed upon her and Marley wanted to say she did not like potato puffs, but her breath caught in her throat. She heard herself say, "I own a potapus."

It was not her mother's face that came close to hers and asked her to respond to abrupt questions about her body. Someone else had found her. She was being rescued. She did her best to answer this person. "Yeth. No. Ow! It hurths."

Marley was remembering when the tent began to slip and she had reached after it, how frightened she was that she would lose it because

Shute would be mad at her and never do favors for her again. Like her father. And now Dannel. She was remembering when she began to fall, all she could think of was to push herself away from the truck so it's big wheels would not run over her. Shute's tent had fallen with her. Again and again it slid under her and rolled with her. Now, it was the funniest thing. To see Shute's squirrelly little face looking at her in that funny way of his she could not read. "I guts blood on it," she said to him. "But itth all here."

Then Shute was stroking her face. Pushing her wet hair away from her eyes. Talking to her. What he said did not register in her pain ridden body. Just that he wasn't mad at her. And she was no longer mad at him.

pEARL

Pearl felt weak over what had to be done to help this girl. "All we can do is stop the bleeding. Rescue is almost here, Marley. Hang in. We'll need shelter, Clyde. Can you prop up the tent? Shute, stop fondling her and help Clyde!"

fLY

Fly was the first to yell at Dannel. He grabbed at the yellow rope and felt the slack before he saw his nephew's possible last seconds of life. Anyone in rescue knows not to use the yellow rope. Yellow ropes were for flares. Like a drunken sailor, Fly held onto the rope. Frozen from emotion. Gulping at air. It was remarkable. That cheer. Josh pumped him on the back. Hard. Fly fell on his knees. His hands slid across the railing. Then Josh was beside him. Not saying a word, just there. Fly knew what he meant. "God damn, Josh. When something like that ... when it comes along ... so quick ... well, God damn! Ain't nothing like it. But I tell you what. If I had the druthers, I'd swear you in as deputy so I can get back to the van and sleep this thing off."

The boy said quietly, perfectly, in a reasonable voice, "Me, too, Fly. Me, too. But the thing is, we came this far, we saw, and now we gotta conquer. That's reality."

Rescue had men with equipment on the ground. Working with Marley. The stretcher was there, too. Another one was being sent down for Dannel and one for Shawn. Fly got to his feet. "You're right, Josh. We got a job to finish. Stay close. I can use a straight thinker. God knows I can use all the help I can get."

jOSH

Moments before, Josh had felt helpless. Like he was going along for the ride. Just as he put his hand on Fly's shoulder, the whole scene around him no longer overwhelmed him. In fact, it gave him a powerful feeling. This rescue thing. How all the pieces seemed to fit together. How good it felt to see it happen. He had not thought Fly to be an especially keen man. He was a cop, after all. A very tired cop, who had a job to do and got it done the best he could. Josh felt it easy to have respect for a man like that.

On the ride back, sitting beside his injured friend, he remembered Dannel's mother. Mrs. Harris knew the seriousness of Marley's note. Not him, or Dannel. She knew what to do. Fly, Vern, Shute. They'd do the same for anyone. Perhaps even Arnold. Josh could give him that. And Billy. What was Billy's story? Josh had not noticed anything special about the man when he'd seen Billy at Ellen's. 'Cept maybe, Billy didn't trust him. Josh could work on that, too.

lEN

Along about supper time, Len Harris phoned his wife only to get the answering machine. "Sorry I'm late, Sally. Something's come up. One of my students. That drug head girl I told you about. She got lost somewhere up by the Loop. I'm stopping at the fire station to see how the search is going."

Len Harris did research for his non-fiction book every Saturday at the State Library in Augusta. On his way back to Crossing Place, he decided to get a ham sandwich and coffee at the truck stop while he waited for the rain to pass. He sat at a table where he could watch the news report on Channel five. There was Billy Trent at the firehouse talking about Marley.

Len knew her impulsiveness would get her into real trouble one of these days. He finished his sandwich before he called Sally. A half hour later, Len Harris was being told by Billy how his impulsive son was lucky to be alive.

cINDER

Sometimes thoughts spill out of our brain pockets and are lost before we have time to explore them. Cinder had submitted these words as part of her next column. A few hours later, she had let her students know she wasn't seasoned enough to have all the answers. A few hours after that...as Billy had pointed out ... she was witnessing people showing the courage and wherewithall it took to reach out to someone in need at a cost to themselves. What made them do that? It was not an unattached thought. For Cinder's thoughts flashed over her nightmare of being trapped under a waterfall and a man in overhauls reaching for her. Long ago, when she was four. Saved her from drowning. Who he was, she did not know. Billy was right. You never know about people. When troubles come, a common thread seemed to pull people together. It was a natural thing for them to do. It was just as natural for them to go back about what they were doing when the threads were no longer holding them together. Before word came that Marley was being lifted out of the chasm, Cinder had people lined up to help the Crockers plus volunteer with the local Youth Group. Maybe, she thought, the bond that started here could lead to lasting friendships. Not forgotten before each had a chance to explore them.

sALLY

Sobs tore out of Jayne's depth while Sally repeated Fly's words to Jayne as he spoke them into the phone Sally held tightly to her ear. "Fly says to tell you that she is in one hell of a mess. Hanging onto life like a trooper. Er, pardon his French. She's bruised, broken, and torn up. Bandaged, and braced, and poked with needles. They have her in the Ambulance now. He doesn't know if she is paralyzed or if her legs are broke or missing. Sorry girl. He's so glad she's alive, he can't hold anything back. The rain has passed over and everyone is coming home! 'Cept Shute and two of his volunteers. They plan to head back to Shute's jeep. Fly says you can just guess what they'll be doing in a couple of hours. Fly, Josh, Spaulding and Dannel are driving behind the ambulance. And Shawn somebody. Dannel will tell us about him. Watch the news because there's filming going on as we speak. Arnold, he thinks. Arnold done good, he says. Arnold's having a helicopter come to the airport to wait for the ambulance. Marley may be heading to Bangor or Boston. Get Jayne and Ted out there to go with them. You got a spit over thirty minutes."

Sally clicked off the phone. Both Ted and Jayne came to her and gave her a hug. Jayne calmly asked Sally to help her pack the things she and Ted would need. Overnight things. Money. A list of phone numbers. Medicine. Clothing. Sally was relieved when Phil and Beatrice insisted on driving the Crocker's to the airport.

Other volunteers arrived to help Sally close down the Crocker's house. Then Sally went home and crawled into her feather bed. She worried for Josh and Len. Dannel, she knew, could always take care of himself. Exhaustion made her sleep.

lEN

Len sent a bandaged and bruised Dannel to his room so as not to alarm his mother. He knew what she had been through on this day. Billy Trent let him know how good it was of her to stay with Jayne and Ted. Keeping the lid on things. Sally was asleep. Still dressed. Len lowered his heavy body onto the bed and put his arm around her. "You done good," he said. "You put in quite a day. I'm proud of you, Sally."

Sally turned so her head was stuffed into his shoulder. She was sobbing! "Oh, Len. It was so hard. Jayne and Ted. So different. To wait for word. Their child, you know. I couldn't leave. They seemed to be as lost as she was. I didn't know how it hit me until I crawled into bed.

"Well, I guess this is as good a time to tell you as any." Len's voice was soft, "Billy Trent said you were a silent hero. I guess he meant the kind that goes unnoticed."

Sally lifted her head and said, "If you spoke to Billy, do you know if Fly is bringing Josh and Dannel home?"

"I took them. Dannel takes after you. Over did it a little today. He's quite shook up. Only ten o'clock, already asleep!" Len let the rest of the story wait until morning. He didn't quite know how to tell her anyway.

kEVIN

"Ach. Wait. Be right there." First he had to get orientated. The room was dark and he wasn't dressed. And Frieda was missing. The knocking stopped while he wrapped himself in a blanket and found the light switch. He opened his bedroom door to Ellen's white face. He supposed his own face was no less white.

"She's alive, Mr. Young. Would you believe it? And wait 'til you hear about Dannel. Go back to sleep. I just wanted to let you know that Marley's on a plane and on her way to a Boston hospital. Isn't that great? Good night. See you in the morning."

Yes. It was great. But he couldn't get to sleep right away. He had to count his blessings.

dANNEL

"Sorry. Was the TV too loud? I didn't mean to wake you."

His mother shook her head. " 'S OK. I want to hear. I'll just fetch some coffee."

She did not move. Dannel waited.

"Did you get a haircut, or something? Something's wrong with your head."

"Don't worry, Mom. I only got five stitches. You should've seen Shawn. Two broken ribs and two black eyes. That's what you get doing miracle things. Least wise that's what Fly says. When Marley was drug up the mountain, she looked much worse than me. Josh said she won the ugly contest, but I won the medal for stupid."

114

His mom was looking at him stupidly. He clicked off the TV. "The news will be on again at six. Let's get some coffee and I'll tell you all about it."

"Your father said you over did it." Even without coffee her voice sounded clear.

So Dannel told her. About the convoy ride up to the Loop and the radio conversations. Headlights and TV cameras. People sliding down on the ropes and the little people doing a dance down below in the rain. The excitement that Marley was found alive. How it made Josh sick. How he wanted to help, but fell instead.

"Shawn and Fly will be on the news. And some pretty awful pictures of Marley. They don't know if they can save her legs. A bear chewed on them. You know, they get hungry this time of year. Don't usually attack humans. They must have smelled the blood. Marley fell a long way. Fell off a truckload of timber. Just like that spill some years ago, they say. Same place, too. Busted her up, but good."

"Stop," ordered his mother. "Who is Shawn? Was he with Marley? And how did you fall? For crying out loud, young man. Give me details I can relate too."

They carried their coffee to the livingroom.

Dannel told her about the rope. He told her Shawn had broken his fall. "The news will tell it like there were three rescues. Shawn was in all of them."

His mother leaned across the couch and hugged him. "This one's for you, Babe." She kissed his forehead. "This one's for Shawn. Shouldn't hug a man with broken ribs.

"What were you doing when all this was going on?"

"Waiting. At Crocker's."

"Fly had said something about waiting. That there was to be a lot of it." Dannel smiled at his mother. "You are the best, Mom. I'm glad you're in my corner. I know Mrs. Crocker appreciated your help." He was surprised when she said Crocker did, too. He'd not thought of Crocker.

115

cINDER

A newswoman asked Fly, "What do you think she was doing up here alone?"

Fly didn't let her have that question. "I don't get inside the heads of teenagers. They maybe don't think things through because they ain't worldly enough."

Fly had more to say; but there it was. The thought Cinder couldn't quite get to. Worldly. Not seasoned, not being old and ripe, not experienced, not being better. He meant aware. In the world you were in. For teenagers it would be in the eye of a storm. Everyone watching to see how they turned out. If they got out. Because of Fly's simple words, she could almost understand something for the first time. About Marley.

Seconds later, Cinder was reaching out to Carla via the internet. Asking why she had seen Marley as a problem instead of seeing Marley as someone with a problem.

aMY

This was a day Crossing Place would remember for a time to come. Everything that happened to the people in this town affected Amy. Billy. My goodness, Billy. Back in the swing after all that time. Sometimes one never knows. And Shute! Selfish little bastard. Who'da guessed he'd come through like that? Yet she knew better, didn't she? Oh, and Cinder Smythe. So young. Trying not to be. Cinder seemed overcome with her inner feelings when the search came to a close! Amy wondered what *The Chatoyant's* take on this would be. What effect this had on the teachers and adults in this small community who both admired and rejected little Marley as a lost cause, on the students who clung to every word? What must Marley's action mean to them? What of Sally and Jayne? Both with injured children. And Fly. She had to hand it to him. Jumping on Marley's note, but not mentioning it on TV. She heard him say every search was worth it. She heard him say, "I like not being disappointed."

"Neither do I, Fly," she said aloud. She wept then. For little Marley. For Rachel and Vern. For Frieda, Kade, and Dean. For Kevin, too. Frieda had told Amy what he said to her. About a person's not knowing what they will do until a situation happens. She wept for her own lost child. For the loss she felt for her. Amy never wanted to be caught off guard again; yet she often was. One couldn't logically plan for unknowns.

It was close to noontime before Amy was able to drop her deep thoughts. To admit the truth. That most surprises were good ones. No matter how small. And she was due.

sHUTE

Clyde and Pearl fawned over Shawn. All Shute said was, "You done good, man. Tell that wife of yourn, we're plumb proud of you." Being hauled up on ropes was not in Shute's repertoire. He stood helplessly by when the three injured people were lifted up to the railing. Thankful that the rain had stopped by now. What amazed Shute was that when all the equipment and people that came with it were up and gone, two people stood beside him to watch them go.

"I'm not about to join in on that. I'm walking back to your jeep." Said Clyde.

"Me, too," said Shute. "Might be safer. Some of those people were crazy."

"Me? I need the space a good walk can give me. I ain't facing any cameras. Would like some coffee, though." Pearl had sorted out their gear, shouldering hers.

"All I gots is beer and some fixings."

They all seemed in agreement over that offering.

"Anyway, Shute, that there mound over there is your tent. I'll take the first carry."

"Good man," said Shute, stretching himself to ready his muscles for the trek back.

"And what am I, Shute?"

"Dammed if I know, Pearl. If'n you don't mind, I'd say you are the best man amongst us." Shute looked at Clyde whose broad smile seemed to agree.

"OK! Let me know when it's my turn to carry the tent, and we'll see about that."

After a beer and sandwiches, the three rescuers became quite chatty. They sat around a fire; so, as in most cases where there was fire and beer, there was talk.

"By the way, Shute, is there another name you got?" Asked Clyde.

"Grover. It's Grover Shute."

"Oh, the rock business place. They say you ain't no family man," mused Pearl.

"I had family around here oncet. A half brother. Sylvester Shirly. I called him Lester-the-pester. He married Amy. She's my half sister in law." Shute peered out from under the brim of his hat. "We're just acquaintances, you know. But I can trust you, right? Would take it kindly if'n you didn't mention that. Especially to Amy."

"You related to Amy Shirly? The greenery goddess?"

"Don't call her that, Clyde. She being my half sister in law from years back."

"How come I don't know this, Shute?"

"Well, Pearl, if'n you knows anything, you knows Lester Shirly run off and left her, he did. I come here to find him. Hoped he'd come back. Never did. Amy was sick for a time. Then her father died and she had a brother to raise. Guess she's still married to the pest. Kept his name. I never asked. Thought I would some day. She's the only family I got in these parts. In fact, she's the only family I got outside of Lester. Wherever he is. Never really liked him, though. Did his father."

"I knowed you was friendly with Amy," said Clyde. "I see you together at Murphy's sometimes."

"She doesn't know about me. Everyone around here calls me Shute. I just left it at that. I help her out sometimes. It's more than a business arrangement to me. Don't know why I'm laying this all down on you. About my brother. I'd sure not like Amy to know."

Pearl was not convinced. "Don't see why you need to hold anything back, Shute. You weren't the one who took Amy's baby. That no good brother of yours did."

Shute's mouth fell open. "Baby?"

"Amy had a baby?" Clyde seemed to be as surprised as Shute.

"I thought he left here to find work. Oh, for God's sake. Now I really don't like him. Let me see. When I got out of the Navy, I come here to look for him. I'd been sending him money. When I found out about Amy, I asked Fly ...."

"OK. So you went to the police?"

"Fly said he had searched some for him. Couldn't tell me much. Now, here's a man who put in quite an effort to find a kid on the mountain. But, if my brother had a kid, why didn't he do the same for Amy's little one?"

"One of us should ask him, Shute." Clyde seemed serious.

"That didn't seem to work before," said Pearl. "I suggest we all get together and ask him."

"I'll drink to that," said Shute. He lifted his beer to his lips; but did not drink. Pearl was looking at him. Looking into his soul.

"What? Now what?"

"Amy," said Pearl. "She knows. As most people probably do. You've been around here long enough to understand that there are some things people don't talk about, yet they know. They probably know what you are up to. Have been up to all these years. Some of the older folk are still waiting to see what you'll do. You can count on this. Amy knows. She knows just about everything that goes on in this town."

"Yep. I've heard that said at Murphy's. She's an intriguing lady." Clyde nodded his head and turned his eyes away from Pearl and Shute.

Shute teased Clyde, "I thought you said she was a goddess."

"I still think she is and don't tell her I said that. I admire her pluck. OK?"

"Look. We should call it a night. Suppose there's room at The Post?" Pearl did feel tired. She was sure she could sleep round the clock.

119

"Yeah. I got a key," said Shute. "I'll get us in. Get a good night's sleep. If I can sleep. I sure got a powerful spat of thinking to do."

"Me, too," offered Clyde. "A bed sounds better'n a hard cot in the back of my truck."

It was Pearl who picked up and doused the fire before they left.

fARLEY

When Arnold got through interrogating Farley, he didn't know which end was up. Except for knowing he wanted to get a hold of Shute. Arnold said Farley was lower than the pot he pissed in. All Farley had done was not take Shute's warning as seriously as it turned out he should have. He let the girl eat all the chicken casserole she wanted. It was a natural thing for him to ask her to smoke outside. He thought he was treating her decent. Besides, where'd she go if she didn't have a ride?

"I thought Big Al was heading North. Wrong direction for the girl to hitch a ride home."

"You make sure of it?" Arnold's face was redder'n a rooster's cock.

"No. While he gassed up, my wife had a problem with the stove. I went to calm her down. Big Al just paid for his gas and drove off. The girl stayed outside. A car drove up and left. I supposed it was the girl's mother."

"Well, it weren't. She never made the call. Big Al went South. You let that girl slip through your fingers and never even gave it a second thought! I should have your license for this!"

"I...."

"Don't say anything that can get us all in trouble. Hear?"

Farley kept low as he was told. It was not a problem. What with all the people running in and out and getting supplies and making phone calls. License? No brown bagging, power grabbing, swell headed Game Warden was gonna put his greedy fat hands on Farley's license, Farley's livelihood, or Farley's wife's cooking even if he had to run a campaign all the way to the Supreme Court! Farley was run ragged throughout the day. Near dark, when the commotion subsided, Arnold swaggered in.

"Farley, I gotta hand it to ya. You did good. Sorry I got you all riled up. I over reacted. Did the same to Shute. And he up and put me in my place! I'm a sorry son of a bitch, Farley. I don't deserve to be in charge of search and rescue. Tell you what, though, I'm gonna work my butt off to deserve it. And the first place I want to start is to smooth things over with you. Hell, man! I had no right to get on you like that. As if ...."

"Whoa!" said Farley. "Sit your sorry ass down, Arnold. I ain't got the energy to listen to anymore of your jawing. Why don't you have a plate of my wife's stew? It'll give your mouth something more satisfying to do. It's on the house. For the way your search turned out. Helen makes a great stew."

Later, Farley made peace with Shute. Served stew to him and Clyde and Pearl. Let them use the back room to sleep off what had happened that day. Later he told Helen that he knowed why that girl didn't call her mother. The pay phone was out of order.

cINDER

Carla's response to her fuddled thoughts made Cinder feel like the ant whose high hopes went toward lifting a rubber tree plant.

Hi, Cinder. So you missed on Marley, the bird in the bush. I don't know how your mind thinks, yet its output twists toward the warm and positive. Therein is your strength, Cinder. Make no mistake about that. You kept on with your plans after Rudd left. Your response column is a good thing. Not for everyone, but for those whose feelings swing high and low on the agenda of life. They are ready for inspiration. It's not like you are shoving it down their throats. I work with people who need to re-color their experiences. Your words are helpful to them, sometimes healing. Who knows why? Perhaps it's the ownership. A more positive step than beating themselves up over a past experience.

There's no magic wand. There is a Chatoyant! *CARLA of the 3 C's*

tHE cROCKER's

Jayne checked the connections to Marley's fluid intake and the color of the fluid in her urine bag before patting at Marley's hair and kissing her forehead. "You look lovely today, my dear. I'm so proud of you for being so brave. Just try to be brave a little longer. We will know soon about your left leg. The doctor is waiting for your vital signs to stabilize before he operates again. All I want you to do is rest. We'll be here for you. One of us will always be here. I love you, Marley. Josh says to tell you, you done good. He and Dannel are the reason we found you so quickly. They must be two of your best friends." She hoped Marley could hear her. Hear the love she had for her. If only love could heal her beautiful daughter.

Crocker cupped Marley's hand in his and held his tongue as his wife babbled away. He wanted to say how pleasant their daughter's face seemed when she wasn't lying or yelling at them. He wanted to tell her he was sorry that he had let anger happen between them. He prayed silently that she would be alright. She deserved better. He vowed to see she got the best care they had to give her.

As much as she wanted to, Marley could not talk to her parents. She did not know how to tell them about the pain she was feeling before her accident. Once she had thought her parents did not care. She had hated them for letting her go on and on like that. Their not telling her the truth. About Teddy. Why they did not get along. Her mother was not his mother. His father was not her father. Sometimes she wished it the other way around. But, here Teddy's father was, beside her mother and loving her. She decided not to hate them anymore. She decided to let them care over her for as long as she could. Anyway, the medication made her drowsy. Why fight it?

fRIEDA

"No," said Frieda when Ellen offered to call her mother to the phone. "I can only talk a few minutes. I thought about you when I saw the story about Marley on the TV. I just wanted you to know that it set me to task thinking about that poor mixed up young thing. No one really knows what others are thinking. Remember the mud pies Kade and Dean made for you? The fat, juicy mud pies Dean and Kade laid down on your history report? You said, 'It's not everyone who enjoys mud pies like I do.' Then you set those pies in the sun to bake and said, 'Wait and see. When they are done, we will see something scientific.' And when they saw them dry to dirt that was easily brushed off your paper so it was just fine again, the look on their faces made us all laugh. What happened to Marley is far from being funny. But it's the thing about waiting. Waiting to see something we don't need to wait for anymore once it's in the open. Am I making sense? If problems were like mudpies, we could find a way to laugh about them. Can you imagine seeing everyone who walks around your school who does drugs or alcohol or worries too much having dried dirt on their hands?"

Ellen's soft, little laugh stopped Frieda's rambling. "That would be funny."

"I just wanted...wanted you to not feel responsible, Ellen. That's all. Not hide your feelings, either. Whoops. I got caught. They say to stop talking."

"Bye," said Ellen. "Keep your hands clean."

Frieda hoped that Ellen's words meant she had not overstepped. To her caregivers she asked, "Is there some way I can have a pen and paper? I have a poem to write."

kEVIN

Kevin found her asleep. She was holding a pencil. A pad of paper was on the bed beside her. Frieda had written,

"Sometimes we think people are as fragile as soap bubbles until we see the rainbow inside of them."

He waited for her to awake so he could talk with her about that. While he waited, he read another poem she had written. He wondered if it could work for Marla, too. He planned to ask her when she awoke. He knew she would like that and it pleased him. Then he read the poem again and realized her poem had meaning for him, too. A personal one.

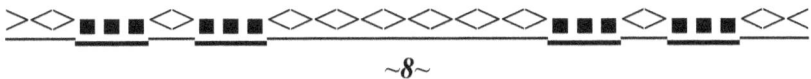

~8~

!***Knowing what to do is part of a growth thing***.*Chatoyant*(Shaw-toy-awnt)!

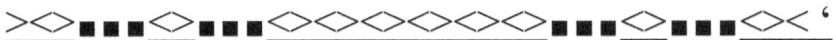 '

eLLEN

Monday was not a compulsory day of school. Due to Marley's accident and the uproar it caused around town, students who wanted counseling could check in at will. There were no regular classes. Just group meets and some pick up games. Volleyball, soccer, and basketball. Time for laughter as well as feeling blue. Free sandwiches and juice in the cafeteria. Crocker was also there. Walking aimlessly around the corridors. Talking to students and asking if they were OK. Ellen saw him more as a father who had come close to losing his daughter than as a principal here to help grieving students. She touched his arm. "Mr. Crocker. Everything's fine here. Why don't you go home? Get on back to Marley? You could use a shave. Maybe a hot bath and some chicken soup. They have take out at Murphy's. Shall I call for you?"

Easy as that. Before Ellen got off the phone with Rachel, a chum whom Ellen played with since she was six, Crocker had left.

A basket had been set up by the front office. A card bearing Marley's name was tied with a large yellow ribbon that hung from the handle. It was minutes before nine o'clock and cards, candy, and gifts already overflowed onto the table. Ellen felt so moved by this audacious day, she went into the art room to log her thoughts onto paper. In a cartoon strip. Perhaps for Marley. She began with the note. She drew the scene from The Loop to the chasm, all cluttered with rescuers. And what Dannel must have looked like repelling from the rope. And Josh leaning over the railing looking angry.

Shawn below about to save him. Shute's tent with Marley inside. She drew the media ... cameras and talking reporters and a smattering of people jumping out of cars and running to help ... as small and mighty. She did the same for a busy scene at the firehouse, Fly on TV, the ambulance heading to the airport, and students milling around the school corridors. She drew Crocker as a giant who towered over them. She gave him a bulbous nose and had him carrying a rumpled handkerchief and pulling a wagon with a sign that read 'No free rides.' The wagon held ribbons, candy bars, and pamphlets about drugs.

When she finished, she stepped back to look at her work, and almost stepped into Ms Elliot, the art teacher.

"Young lady," Ms Elliott said, speaking in a clip above stern. "What is this? Where did it come from? What have you been doing?"

Ellen always felt intimidated by Ms Elliot. She was so direct and critical and demanding. "I was only..." she began.

"Forgive me, Ellen. I like what you have done. I'm not faulting you. I just wonder where all this talent came from. You've never shown me anything like this before. You've captured an earmark! A spirit. I have one suggestion. Instead of the note, put in the plane. Then I will go with you, with your mother's permission, to submit this work to the newspaper. While you make your finishing touches, I'll call your mother to get her OK. Miss Smythe has student letters she thinks will have publishing value. Your art work is the prize. Be about a half hour."

Ellen cleared the box lines in her drawing. Dispersed tall trees throughout the empty spaces. Took away the note and put in a sketch of a half closed window. Drew in a bed and slippers. And a very large alarm clock. She changed her rendition of Crocker to have a tearful, happy look; and the wagon into the card filled basket bearing Marley's name. Then she set the plane above all the activity below. Banking away from rain clouds in the West. She even found room for Shute's jeep with the three volunteers bursting out of the windows. Ellen titled her full page spread: "Crossing Place: No one really knew if a search for Little Marley would bring her home alive, until they did."

aMY

Wanting to know. Waiting to know. How could someone, so young and innocent know how terrible it was to be caught off balance over something one never thought about happening? Over something that would change a life forever? How a whole town was caught off guard? Amy clipped Ellen's piece out of the paper. It captured her feelings exactly. Gave her balance. She knew she was not alone in that. And in the plane? Thanks to God, another kind of hero was there! Vern.

cINDER

Cinder sat looking out her window at the mountain. Thinking over Carla's message. The battery powered wall clock ticked off time. Its pendulum swung to and fro. Its hands traveled in circles. By and by she envisioned the hands to be paint brushes. Changing the colors as they revisited the same place in circles. So there it was. Carla had set her up for it. A way to foster worldliness. How simple! Cinder thought out a question to ask her readers: ***Do you have an experience upon your life palette that colors your reactions now? Let's share and care over it.*** Cinder broached her idea to Allyson by saying it would broaden the scope of her column.

Allyson was delighted to add a Life Palette spot to *The Chatoyant* column. "It sounds corny, but it fits."

The plan was to have the new spot ready for the Thanksgiving issue. Cinder began right away to lay the groundwork. She wrote:

Knowing what to do is part of a growth thing. As we go down the aisle of our lives, we sometimes are option shopping. If we miss one, hindsight counters with, 'Why didn't I think of that?' As though it were possible all along. Perhaps so. Sometimes thoughts just pop into our heads and we don't know where they came from. It's a good thing when we can hold onto them long enough to cash them in. When the time is right and we see their value.

mARLEY

Having a visit from Miss Smythe made Marley feel better about herself. She had not expected to laugh about the confusing thoughts she had while waiting to be rescued; yet, there they were being giddy.

"I think there's a big difference between a bear and a mosquito, Marley. If it were me...flat on my back and no way to run? I'd take the mosquito. As Vern Paselli said, 'Don't argue with a bear! Outsmart him!' Of course, I don't ever want to be out after dark with one."

"Yeah, right! You'd walk right up to him and tell him his time was up."

"I used to be afraid of the dark. I had nightmares of being trapped under a waterfall."

"You mean drowning?"

"Oh, Marley. You're so smart. Yes. You fell off a truck. I almost drowned. I floated out of a car in the river. This man in overhauls saved me. I think. He could have been a dream. I don't know. I was only four years old. I wanted my mother."

Marley began to understand something. Something about her own experience. "I threw up, and didn't know I was bleeding all around my head and chest. I wanted my mother, too. I closed my eyes so she could find me in the dark."

"Yes. To be safe. I thought this man gave me a lollipop; but it could have been my thumb. I sucked my thumb until I started school."

"All I remember about falling is holding onto the tent. I pushed off so I wouldn't fall under the wheels of the truck. At least, I thought it was the truck. It must have been the railing. I don't remember rolling down the embankment. I rolled around the tent."

"I wonder if Dannel remembers rolling around with Shawn!"

"Are you still afraid of water?"

"No. When I was eight, my foster mother told me about the accident. Her telling me that got me over the fear of swimming lessons. I learned to swim. I have a decent side stroke. And I float real good."

"I thought my mother was playing hide and seek with me. I wanted her to pay attention and there she was. Right there with me. Until the pain came and woke me up."

Miss Smythe got all quiet then. "Mine wasn't."

"She died?" Asked Marley.

"My father died. In the accident. My mother didn't want me. I lived with other families."

"Like Ellen."

"Ellen? You mean with the Young's?"

"I mean with Mrs. Mitchell. She and Sammy. I wonder if Ellen was ever afraid of the dark? I wonder if she ever wanted to run away. Did you? Want to find your mother?"

"I found her. Before she died."

Marley's heart hurt inside her small chest. "Was she happy to see you?"

"Yes. She really liked my hair. And my coat. And my boy friend. And didn't remember me. She was very sick. I'm glad I saw her, though. She was funny. I like that."

"I like that, too, Miss Smythe. My mother is sick. She has headaches. I guess it could be worse."

"We both know something about worse. I have to go, but...know this. Beauty is in the eye of the beholder. I behold you and find that to be true." Miss Smythe placed a small book in Marley's hand, and left quietly.

Tied to the binding of it was a silver pen. Marley read the *Chatoyant* newspaper column taped to the inside cover. It was about options, hindsight, and cashing in on the values in life. Under it, Miss Smythe had written, "What?" in bold letters. The book was blank. Marley thought aloud, "What indeed!" She wrote this on the first page:

"I think my mother is beautiful. She is the soft in my heart. She is the hope in a darkened room. She is love to a family. She is my mother. I love her."

The thing was, Marley could not remember saying these words to her mother. That was then. She felt the value of them now. Some day soon she would share them with her mother. And her father. Not her blood father, but her real one. She would write other thoughts as they came to her. She had a lot of thoughts to cash in on. In particular there was one of Dannel. And one for Farley. And Shute? What About Shute? She did not know what to think of Ellen.

eLLEN

"It's a little thing really, Marley. But...."

"Shh on that Ellen. It's important and you know it. I can see it in your eye! I may have a probably crippled leg, but my head isn't lost to the world ... now. In fact, Ellen, my brain is getting stronger and I see a glimmer of pride in that eye of yours. Show me!"

Ellen unfolded the newspaper she had brought to give to Marley.

"Oh, my God! Ellen! This is beautiful! Is this my father? Did he cry? This puts things in perspective for me, Ellen. Crossing Place and Little Marley all in a row! Wait. Who could have drawn such a rendition as this?" When Marley read the by-line, she dropped the paper and spread her arms for Ellen for a hug.

"I didn't know I had it in me, Marley. To create such a thing. Neither did Ms Elliot. She's the one who got me to ask the paper to print it. She and Ms Smythe. I even got paid for it. But this is not all I have to share. It's from Frieda Young. You know, Mr. Young's wife? She had to go to the hospital just before we knew you were missing. It was bad. She coulda died, just like you. And she wrote a poem about living through it. She thought you might like it."

I got hold of something today.
I think they call it life.
Yesterday is gone. And here I am again.
Looking forward to what's next.
This may not be a great game,

But I'm on a great team.
'Cause Daddy calls it Team Frieda!

Together, Marley and Ellen dissected it. Then Marley shared what she knew about Ms Smythe and how the poem fit her, too.

dANNEL

The Patriots were doing great. How about that defense? Seeing a football game was the main focus for Thanksgiving as far as Dannel was concerned. He and Josh were taping the game for Marley as they had promised. At the half, Dannel's father went to get the sandwiches his mother made for them. So Dannel and Josh talked about the news reports of how the President had somehow scooted past the secret service men and hightailed it to Iraq to feed the troops. Well, a few dozen of them.

"Not even the President's parents knew? As if!" Snorted Josh.

"An ex president being stood up." Nodded Dannel.

"Making plans he didn't keep."

" Well, that was his back up plan."

"Yeah. Shows he can make plans."

"Yeah, well, as a cover up. Would make a James Bond movie."

The young men looked at each other to say, "Nah," in each others face as Dannel's Dad brought in the sandwiches.

"I can take these back."

"Dad. If you want the truth? Not a good back up plan."

cINDER

The Three C's spent Thanksgiving together at Charissa's upstate New York campus home. Cinder brought fresh pressed Maine cider and a blueberry relish. Carla brought a twisted loaf of walnut, cinnamon, and raisin bread along with a pot of Boston Baked Beans. Charissa had a fine stock of Vermont Cheese, cranberries, pumpkin pies and the largest turkey Cinder had ever seen. "Are we going to be able to eat all this?"

"No, my dear. We are going to eat the stuffing," postulated Carla.

Charissa laughed. "I had to do turkey. When people drop by, I can offer them left overs. But today, we can have a sneak treat."

"Works for me. Do you have any fries?" Cinder asked with a cautious laugh.

"Oh, can we talk without them? I'm on a diet," said Carla.

"We're always on a diet," reminded Cinder. "But I was only kidding. Anyways, with all this fresh air, we can walk off an elephant."

"And someone special will be coming for desert. He's at his folks for dinner. Be here around six or so. We probably won't be talked out by then. First, let's tour the house."

The first floor rooms were big, with high ceilings and plenty of windows to let in the light. Color abounded everywhere. In the rug, curtains, and scatter pillows, on the overstuffed chair and couch. Art pictures hung from the warmly painted walls. Magazines and books covered parts of the huge wall of shelves in the den which also held a formidable looking computer set up.

Upstairs, the rooms were graced with different color schemes in period settings

"You can choose your room," said Charissa. "I thought Cinder would like the Victorian with it's endowment of crisp lace curtains and intriguing red satin coverlet. And Carla would like the English Tudor design. It comes with a chaise lounge and a lap desk!"

"I love this bathroom," gaped Cinder. "It's bigger than my whole apartment."

"Where's the washing machine?"

Charissa opened white louvered folding doors to reveal the well designed laundry unit. "It's the real reason I wanted this house, Carla. After all those years of struggling with a laundry bag up all those stairs."

"And you did all this yourself?" Cinder was not only incredulous, she was pleased.

"No. Most of it. The basics ... floors, walls, accouterments ... were fine. I just added. The paintings. Mine. Curtains. I made. Couch and chair and table set. I borrowed. Beds. Came from friends. Who use them sometimes. I bought fine china and sterling ware. I invested in cleaning supplies...including a vacuum that practically runs itself...and I have a live-in student who cleans when she can. Her room is Old New England. She's gone home to North Carolina for Thanksgiving. My room is furnished in the Quaker style. But as you can see it is quite plush and inviting. The colors are so unique! And oh, Romanoff brings in the groceries once a week. I never want for wholesome food. My classes are a dream. I'm well liked here. I'm in debt, but I am very, very happy. Especially, now we three are together."

"So who's coming for desert?"

"The other owner of this house."

"This doesn't mean ... ?"

"Of course it does. We began dating from the first day I arrived. I told him he'd better watch his step, some woman would be after him. He said he wouldn't mind as long as it was me. We put the down payment on this house in October. We'll be married over Christmas. In Vegas!"

Carla and Cinder squealed with delight and rushed to Charissa for a group hug.

"Can you let us in on a name?" Asked Cinder. "You've named everything else."

Charissa said casually, "I thought I did. Romanoff."

"The grocery boy? He must get a lot of overtime!"

"Professor Romanoff Heppinwhite, Carla. He's an architect. Head of his department."

"Who likes to cook?" Cinder was catching on. "This is starting to be one heck of a holiday. I can't wait to find out what's going on in Boston."

"Me, too," allowed Carla. "The Red Sox are out. The Celtics let go of one of last year's star players. And how about those Patriots?

fRIEDA

What she had thought to be a quaint little get together with her mother turned into one of Frieda's favorite days. At first she thought Ruby and her friend Linda had made a chaos of her livingroom. Chairs were all askew. There were large flowered screens in each corner. Frieda found a chair with clothing thrown across it. Was it her clothing? Her voice came out cross. "Ruby, what have you done?"

"Those old things?" Remarked Ruby in a pandering voice. "Still have a lot of charm, though."

Frieda was stunned to see Linda place some clothes on another chair. So did Ruby. Frieda recognized a quilted vest she'd seen Ruby wear with an olive skirt.

"Linda and I have spent hours getting everything ready. Instead of a shopping spree ... which you are not ready for ... your mother and I decided we would have a clothing fest. It's like shopping in a bargain basement. Except all you need is something to trade. We have herbal tea and sweetbreads and trays for holding our cups and plates. Screens behind which to try on clothing. And here come the others."

In they came. Amy, Sally, and Jayne; Frieda's mother with her friends Vida, Beatrice and Molly. All came in carrying garments. They greeted Frieda and Ruby and Linda like long lost friends. Linda filled the stereo with music from the fifties. Ruby showed the ladies how to arrange their bounty on the chairs. When everyone was settled, Ruby and Linda served tea and shortbread.

The ladies gossiped, told jokes, and laughed at them. Soon, Ruby said, "I think we're ready. Remember, value doesn't matter. We'll just go by style. So go ahead and trade what you have for something else." She clapped her hands. "Let the trade-fest begin."

Frieda was quick. She offered to trade her white silk blouse for Ruby's vest. Frieda's mother was quicker. "Oh, my dear. My flowered denim vest would look wonderful with your silk blouse." Victoria offered Ruby a hand detailed leather belt for the silk blouse and asked Frieda for the black scarf that had a chipmunk emblazoned in one corner in exchange for the silk blouse and vest. Frieda now had two vests to go with her silk blouse. She went behind one of the screens to try them on. She almost cried aloud. Her almost flat chest looked sensational!

Amy traded her felted knitted hat for Vida's woven shopping bag.

Jayne and Sally both wanted Molly's heavy red sweater; but Molly liked Ruby's white lace collar and traded for that. "I need it for a bling around my neck." explained Molly. "You know, to please the eye away from my double chin."

So Jayne took Sally's green car umbrella; Sally took Jayne's yellow rain boots. Molly liked Jayne's zippered raincoat and traded a backpack for it. Ruby traded Molly's red sweater to Jane for the backpack. So Jayne got the red sweater. Sally got a yellow sweater from Linda for a reversible wind jacket. Molly traded Jayne's raincoat with Linda for the wind jacket. Jayne and Sally traded sweaters. Molly liked Amy's full length apron with a moose wearing a Santa hat. She traded the wind jacket for it. Jane offered Molly a jogging suit for the apron. Frieda also offered her a jogging suit. Molly liked the apron and kept it.

Beatrice gave Linda three of her dress blouses for a wrap around denim skirt. Then she traded the skirt for Amy's colorfully buttoned woolen jacket. Then she traded the woolen jacket for Frieda's hooded woolen cape. She kept the cape and set about trading her terry bathrobe. "It's new," she said. "And too long."

Ruby gave Beatrice a pair of black corduroy slacks for the bathrobe. "These are not new, but didn't fit either," she confessed.

"Ruby," asked Vida. "Are you planning to shorten that robe?"

"No, It will fit Ellen."

"OK, then," laughed Vida. "I'm trading my two flannel shirts for Frieda's overalls. For my husband."

"Overalls? You giving up on overalls, Frieda?" Amy was skeptical.

"No. Just these. They are big. I could wear two more under them."

"Then you must trade my down mittens for your suspenders."

"Amy, I wasn't trading my suspenders," protested Frieda.

But there they were in her pile of tradeables. She got those mittens!

By the time the music stopped, everyone had something that was new to them. There were a few more trades, however; and most people left with nothing they had come with. First, though, they helped put Frieda's livingroom back in order.

Victoria talked about another clothing fest in the Spring.

Ruby said, "I'm too tired to think about that now."

Frieda was not too tired to write a poem on her very fine day.

Swapping Spree
They came into my parlor
Bearing things they liked but did not need.
And Lo! The trade was on!
Shoes, suspenders, and dresses for shirts, hats, and robes?
Sweaters for overalls or raincoat or backpack?
Two lovely vests to cover my missing breasts?
A fine day it was to give and take all at once
A Trading Spree is so much fun;
I'd recommend it to everyone.

mARLEY

"Then we'll see." The doctor patted her shoulder and left her there upon her hospital bed. Alone, but with her mother and father. The words had not been too encouraging; yet were more than she had hoped for. If the ligaments had healed in her lower leg, a steel brace could be inserted to support her bone. They might be able to save it. If not, they would have to amputate.

Her mother and father were as silent as she.

"I am so lucky," she said. "Just to be alive. My mind is clear. I have wonderful parents and people who love me and care about me. You know, Dad, you could get me a tutor. So I can try to keep up with my studies. I have a lot of free time, you know."

Her father did not argue. In fact both parents seemed overjoyed.

"I'm full of surprises, eh?" The thing was, she surprised herself. When Dannel and Josh mentioned a tutor, she had scoffed at the idea. Her parent's reaction to her decision gave her a warm feeling. Gave her courage that her life was not as lost as her leg.

!Cousins!

---

cINDER

Cinder awoke with a gasp. In the dark, she heard the rushing of the wind outside her window. For a moment she had thought it was water. Was she having the dream again? No. This was different. There was something. Something she saw. Yes. In the painting that hung at the head of Charissa's stairs. Folk Art. Grandma Moses. A village scene. Cape style houses and picket fences. A park. People everywhere. Children playing in a schoolyard. A dog barking at the postman. Men loading bags of apples onto a horse drawn cart. A young couple having a picnic beside a lake. Another couple in a sailboat. Ducks and sheep and horses and cows. A red barn and a white church. A man selling balloons. A mother hen tending her chickens. One chicken had fallen into the lake. Three young ladies under pink and white parasols shyly watched the dapper young man who had plunged his stovepipe hat into the water to rescue it. His coat was slightly opened, exposing his red suspenders.

A man in suspenders had saved her, too. Cinder was sure of it; although there was no mention of him in the newspaper article that Mrs. Jepson, her foster mother, had found for her. "Keep this," she said. "It tells who you are and that you were brave. That you are alive and deserve a good life. Your nightmares come from a bad thing, Cinder. Life is one thing after another. And this is one of them. It is up to you to make it better." Cinder sat up and reached for the extra quilt she always kept at the foot of her bed. The room was warm enough, she did not need it; but she wanted to be comforted by the weight of it. Since talking to Marley of her near drowning, she understood her need to be kept from floating away.

Her childhood thoughts ... that she had been rescued by gallantry and valor ... were the fine and worthy virtues that befit the making of a *Chatoyant*. In fact her column had received many such tales of gallantry and valor. Ellen's cartoon, however, had gone right to the crux of human vulnerability amid a rescue. Allyson was much impressed by the fervor in Ellen's work, liked the message of hope the plane seemed to give. The paper had asked her for more. Ellen drew each one with her trademark plane banking into the mountains, or over lakes, or coming in for a landing. Ellen was paid well for her advertisement work. Charissa was certain Ellen should win an art scholarship. Maybe to upstate New York!

Cinder felt quite settled from her reaction to the suspenders. More than from learning the reason for her nightmares. This was another break through for her. The first time, after reading about her accident, she got into swimming. The Desiderata calmed her over missing Rudd and also enough to write her column. Maybe now she should take up painting! Maybe now she should plan a book as Frieda had done.

The radio announced a no school day. Good enough, thought Cinder, already awake and craving Mumicita's Muffins. She'd get them anyway and surprise Emily. She bounced right on by the uniformed man on the shoveled path. His hand held her arm and turned her toward him. "Smythe?" She heard him say. This could have been a glad moment for Cinder. Except she fainted.

eMILY

The forecast was snow. There had been a mountain of it yesterday. Rain shrunk the banks to almost non existent while she was at work. They'd had a great deal of snow and rain this December. She wondered what last night's storm had left behind. She was not working today, but looked idly out her window to check on the weather. What she saw brought her to her feet. Moments later she was helping a soldier carry a limp Cinder to her apartment.

While he covered her and rubbed her hands, Emily called the High School to say Cinder had fallen on the ice and would not be able to come to work. Instead she heard a recording. No school due to the icy roads.

"Welcome Home," she said to the dark faced soldier. He looked as though he had traveled a long way. "I'm sorry it wasn't sooner."

"I didn't mean to frighten her. The phones were out last night, or I would have called. This morning, I just walked over from the Inn."

Emily got her medical kit and found the smelling salts. She broke the vial and held it under Cinder's nose.

"You're Smythe, aren't you? Are you hurt? How did you get here?"

"Whoa, nice lady. Long story. I'll admit to being Smythe, though. We're related. Tell by the color of our skin."

cINDER

When thoughts came to her brain again, she fought them. "No, no, no," she moaned. Shocked for why this soldier, whom Emily called Smythe, stood on her path. Emily made her sit and face the music. "There's time. No school today."

"I come's as soon as I could bundle up my girl. She's waiting for me at the Inn. Man, did she give me a riding for bringing her here to this ice palace instead of spending my two week leave in New Jersey where the ice melts before lunch." Smythe pulled an envelope from inside his vest. "Just wanted to be sure you got this before Christmas. Special delivery. All the way from the Mid-to-Hell-and-East. My girl and I? We're taking the next available train...er...bus right back to New Jersey. ASAP. Mind if'n I kiss you? So's I can pass it on to the man?"

Cinder spread her arms wide and hugged this man. Kissed him on his right cheek and then his left. He kissed both her cheeks as well.

"I want you to stop that fainting stuff, cousin. You're white enough as it is. Ain't no way for our very own little Chatoyant to behave, now is it? Rudd's letter is best read when you're alone, Angel. Our special little

Chatoyant." Smythe's eyes flashed dark and bright when he spoke. "You know, he's not had a lot of privacy over there."

At last, Cinder came of her own. "This is quite charitable of you, cousin. I would be remiss if I didn't offer you respite until your train awaits. Right, Emily? Grab your coat. Let's feed these brave travelers the best fare in town. Breakfast at Murphy's!"

"Well, sure enough, my dear Chatoyant. And when were you to tell me of this?" Emily whispered these words, yet Smythe heard them.

"OK, no jealousy, now, me ladies. You both look like angels to me." Smythe took each by the arm to escort them toward the Hosteles's Bed and Breakfast to pick up his girl. Take her to that Murphy's place.

"We wait for word every day," said Emily. "I feel so out of touch. It's like oh, yeah. Why am I enjoying this, or planning to do this, when today someone died or was injured in a way I can only imagine? The war is surreal to me. Your being here, Smythe, is like a miracle. I cherish knowing you."

"I'll drink to that," said Smythe seriously. "Now, let's eat and be merry." Smythe did just that. A stack of pancakes, sausage, home fries, scrambled eggs with a smattering of cheese, and two very fine homemade biscuits all on the house. And talked his way through it all.

"I know what you are saying; but, I need to know more of what you are doing than of what I'm doing. Everyday things. Like walking along a busy street and listening to people talk. Like this morning. Shucks. Kids were all lined up at a corner when out pops this woman. You should of seen her. She was wearing a pink hooded parka. I swear to God. And under it was a pink flowered housecoat. I mean, she wasn't even dressed! I could see her boots were too big. She come out to say something to those kids. They jumped up and down and hugged her like she was some kind of heroine. All the while shouting, "No school! No school!" Then the kids took off. Man! What a thing. What a happy thing! I almost went up and hugged her myself."

Beside him his girl Betsy, whom he called Little Bit, her glowing face sparkling without makeup, chimed in jubilantly, "This man, here, is thirsty for the mundane. Through his eyes, little things are completely precious."

Such simple terms. How could she have known? All she knew of Iraq was death and money. Christ, thought Cinder. Blips on the bottom of a TV screen was no excuse for news. Names of dead soldiers were read just last week on PBS. As were the names of the dead from 9/11. Faces of dead soldiers in magazines and local newspapers gave a horrific taste of loss. What was life like for the soldiers there? What was daily life like to the people of an invaded country? Or if the children .... Smythe was right. He needed to see the normal things. And they needed to share them with him. Sharing his side of the story could not help him. So they did. With gentle awareness. Then ... Cinder was alone, reading Rudd's letter. The real Rudd. Honest and strong. Humor covering anger.

"I am sorry, Cinder. Sorry to tell you that your love is all that is keeping me sane. Our first kiss. The way you laugh. The way your hair looks when you take out your braids. The time you got on the dorm roof and tap danced. Always telling me things. Like how I smell and what a good thing it was that I had a flat tire before the bridge that got washed out and had to call you in the middle of the night to say I loved you and might have to swim home to you. You told me to sleep on it. In the pouring rain, no chance for help until morning, and you were worried about my being able to sleep. I bet you are still worried about that. I have no control of what is happening to me. Just to get a letter to you, I have to have my best buddy smuggle it across the border. No mail is let out of this embedded area. None comes in. We eat, scout, stand about, and go to bed. Follow orders. I don't even know the names of my officers. I don't want to know. I don't want to remember them. We've lost twelve soldiers since Tuesday. One got to go home, four got transferred. I don't know how many wounded there were; but the rest died. I volunteer to help the medics whenever I

can. I'm at my best in trying to cheer the guys up. They need to hear words of encouragement so bad, it's like I'm their long lost teddy bear. I'm writing this to you, Cinder, not because I want you to worry, but to tell you I am not a happy trooper and no words can soothe me now. Except those that say I can leave here. I'll need words from your heart then. For a long time. Until I can rationalize what was happening here. Of course, I can write of good things. We made clay marbles. (Big enough to knock someone out if we had to use them for protection.) We sing songs out of tune. (Just so no enemy can get it right.) Kids smile at us. (It's when they aren't smiling that makes us run away from them. Some kids carry bombs. That's how low this war is.) The president came for Thanksgiving. (He didn't know that giving thanks was the last thing on our minds.) I'm so glad that you got to meet Smythe. (I hate that it isn't me.) I've been out of my camp for four days cleaning up another hit spot. So by the time Smythe gets back, our camp may be moved again. The only reason I want Smythe back here with me is that he's your cousin! He makes me feel close to you! I love you, my little Chatoyant. Are you still tasting that relish? Love, Rudd, loving Cinder.
PS - My amulet is in my heart. And it is you!   Rudd"

Cinder felt very close to Rudd then. His letter filled her with a spirit that glistened over her doubts. A spirit that touched those around her and made their every word, every mannerism seem magnificently perfect to her. She let Emily and Racine read Rudd's letter. Thusly, she admitted to them both that she sincerely was Smythe's cousin, albeit by name only. She even confessed that she was truly greatful that they knew she was the *Chatoyant*, saying she would dearly love to have a letter from them to answer. She also confessed that if she needed a base to call home, it would be in Crossing Place because she had close friends here.

And the maiden admitted to the soldier that she was covering her feelings. Her fears. Wishing for things to be fine again. As they once were. And the soldier was thirsty for the mundane. He said he missed those completely precious, every day things. These three words the soldier said to her, "We are cousins." A new truth came to this maiden. Nothing need be as it once was. She had more ahead than behind. That was where she would look. At simple things there for her to see. As much for herself as for all her cousins. Every one!

~9~

!Frieda puts it this way:
"That is the way of life, when it comes, it comes right at you."!

sMYTHE

Crossing Place was less than seventy-miles from the Canadian Border. Of course, he thought about that when he and Little Bit got on the bus and headed South. What was a good two weeks compared to a life of hell? He went against the odds. Took the quality time with Little Bit. His man self wouldn't let him do otherwise. He owed it to Rudd and all the others from whom he'd taken letters home for. Little Bit had mailed the others. She supported his desire to hand deliver Rudd's letter to the *Chatoyant*. What a child! What an angel! He had to go back and tell everyone how close to heaven he'd come by seeing her. How he really felt he was in heaven with Little Bit at his side. Lord a mighty did she make a man feel proud to be hers. There weren't nothing he'd like better'n coming home from hell and marrying this filly. 'Cept maybe a double wedding with Rudd and his angel. Be cousins!

cROCKER

Crocker looked up from his desk when he heard it. The quiet that came from the halls and classrooms. Quite unlike what he'd heard during testing sessions. A sudden, sustained hush. Seconds passed before he stirred himself to cross the space from his small, tidy office space to the front office which was submerged in scattered piles of paper, ribbons and wrappings, boxes, machines, furniture, several staff members, and standing students. Through its windows, Crocker noted the uniformed men entering the front of the building. Hollow tapping sounds from their hard soled shoes echoed their coming his way down the hall.

Racine Elliot slipped from the library and walked with them. She opened the door to the office and stood silently behind them.

The Corporal consulted his clipboard as he spoke in a crisp, well practiced voice. "We are sorry to interrupt your school day. We are looking for a ... Ms Cinder Lorraine Smythe."

A gasp may have come from Racine or himself. They both knew before they heard. Hearing was the hard thing. "Yes," Crocker responded in his Principal's voice. "Come with us." He motioned for Racine to join them in the Teachers' Lounge. So there was no doubt in what would happen next, he said crisply, "We will find her for you. Stay right here."

Around the corner, out of sight of any eyes that would happen to be looking, he stopped Racine. "I am a coward, Racine. I depend upon you to know what to do. I will wait here for you."

Racine's footsteps clicked down the corridor toward Cinder's classroom while he stood against the wall and waited. This wait was as hard for him as it was in waiting to hear news of his daughter ... and that of his son. He said nothing as he opened the door into the Teachers' Lounge for Cinder and Racine. In this face of loss, he noted that Racine was calm and focused. So was Cinder. He, himself, had legs of jelly.

Cinder silently read each of the papers they had for her before placing her signature where it needed to be. Yet she hardly seemed to listen to the apologies offered by the uniformed man and woman. She gave no notice to their quick departure. "Racine," she said in a surprisingly clear voice. "I'm ready." She turned toward Crocker. Her eyes held fast to the knot in his tie. "Take me home, will you Crocker?"

Crocker heard the murmurs break over the building as he walked Cinder outside. Voices buzzed as students changed classes. Lockers banged. Then silence as the movements entered classrooms and doors shut. The only sound then was the roar of his Blazer's engine. And the small, pitiful little moan of the pretty young thing beside him. .

rACINE

Details. Came more quickly to Racine now then they had when she herself had to face what Cinder was facing. Racine's last letter had come after, not before she got the death notice. If Smythe hadn't gotten leave, there never would have been a last letter. Racine felt a small comfort for knowing that. Another thought nagged, but she shook it away. As soon as she got to her classroom, she called Emily's number and left a message. When she saw Dannel's OK sign and relieved face at her classroom door, she again felt comfort. Was it wrong to ask that young man to follow Crocker in Cinder's car? No. He may have joked about botching a rescue mission on the mountain; but he seemed to have accomplished this one without a hitch. After checking to be sure Cinder's lesson plans were in order for the last two schooldays before the Christmas recess ... the last two school days this year ... she made sure Mrs. Kingsbury was free to substitute, to carry Cinder's classes.

eMILY

Stores were open around the clock until Christmas Eve. Even though snow had fallen during the night while she was working, Emily chose to do some last minute Christmas shopping at the mall. When she emerged ... just after nine ... snow was falling again; but the morning sun was visible through the breaking clouds. Emily drove carefully behind a long line of traffic following the snowplow on I-95. The spray of snow from the blades of the plow made it too dangerous to pass. Emily wondered if the Chatoyant would describe it as angel wings, keeping her safe all the way home. So she could sleep. Emily snuggled into her down filled mattress cover to listen to her answering machine. "... and Cinder went right home. I'm sorry to let you know by phone, but I can't get away just yet. I think if you could be there, she would like you to be."

When Emily stood inside Cinder's door, she was surprised to find herself dressed and holding a pot of hot coffee. "This is Emily, Cinder. I'm here. Just here for you." Then Emily sat to drink some coffee and wait for Cinder to need her.

cLYDE

"Mind if'n I join ya?" Clyde slid into the empty chair next to Amy before she could answer. "Just come off a long haul. The snow sure makes it a long one. You closing up after the Holidays?"

Amy moved her newspaper aside as a way to ascertain he was welcome at her table. "I am not. You know better than that, Clyde. Have to keep the fuels burning."

"Yeah, well, what if you wanted to go on a trip? You could hire someone to tend the flock, right?" Clyde knew he'd startled her. Had to. She was edgy these days. Fly had told him why. It was the anniversary of when she'd lost her child and her husband. Pearl explained that to him. How it was a marker in Amy's life. One that holds on and haunts.

"Trip? I ain't venturing out in this weather!"

"Come next week. I got this here haul to do. All the way to Vegas. Of course, I got places in between; but if'n I make good time, I got this two week holdover there. Sure would like to have your company, Amy. Now I knows a week is short notice. There's time, though, to get your doings in order. Listen, I'll check back with you this afternoon. I got me some stuff to do. Meet you here around five? We'll have that special dinner I see's Rachel is putting on the menu."

"Hmm," said Amy.

Clyde left Amy at her table as quickly as he'd come. He knew she'd be there at five. Might even be early just to tease. 'Twas her way and he liked it. Shute had forgiven Fly for not telling him about Amy's child. Seems he'd found her safe and settled in a good home and Amy let her be. No point for Clyde to worry over Amy. Although it scared him some, grown man like he was, it had been three years since he'd been to dinner with a woman. Maybe that was enough time to work up an appetite.

rACINE

Emily said it was fine for Racine to talk in a normal voice. "Cinder will hear you anyway. She's awake."

"Hi, Cinder. I brought some stew. It's really cold outside."

Emily made biscuits. Racine set the table.

Cinder came out to eat when it was ready. "Thanks, chums," she said. Her voice was dull, but her body was erect. "My how quickly this day has gone. You not working tonight, Emily? And can you stay, Racine? I'd really like your company. I think there's some caroling going on tonight. I was supposed to join in. I would like to listen when they get to the corner by the maple tree. We will be able to see them from my window."

"We'll both stay," responded Emily. "I think there's enough stew to last three days. Where did you find it, Racine?"

"It's on special at Murphy's. There'll be a call for it tonight."

"Rudd would like this stew. He didn't mention food in his letter. Or wish me a Merry Christmas. It was pretty low over there, I guess."

"Always. Smythe was lucky to get out when he did, I guess."

"What?" asked Cinder.

Racine tried to correct what she had said. "It's that letter you got. You got in time. Time to enjoy it. I know it's better than to have it come after. That was hard for me. I just ... just wonder about ... about Smythe."

"Smythe. I was thinking about him. If I should try to reach him. Right now, I've got to ... go to ... the bathroom."

There was something about the way Cinder said that, that made Racine falter between a sob or a chuckle.

Emily leaned forward to clasp Racine's hand. "It's, OK, Rae," she said with satisfaction. "I've already checked. She's got plenty of toilet paper."

bETSY

When he put down the phone, her man seemed to do so with concentrated perfection. "Damn!" He said almost under his breath. Betsy knew his hug was more for him than for her. She felt his sorrow and hoped it wasn't about his man Rudd. But it was.

"It's awful over there, Little Bit. It's awful hot and dirty and unfriendly. Can't even smile at those people whose country you're in. That ain't the awfullest. No, it ain't."

Betsy knew she had no way to hug out that awful. Only Smythe could do that. He'd written things down for her. For her to read later.

"The awfulest ... the man ... just like that ... I wasn't even there. My man ... gone."

He let go of her then. Walked around the room. Put a mark on her calendar.

"My man's bitch says they told her it was a bomb. In camp. Christ, Bit. He may have been sleeping. Ain't no way you can protect your back when you're sleeping. I thought tho, he wasn't to go back."

She held him, then. Sang to him. A Chicago tune. "Does Anybody Really Know What Time It Is? Does Anybody Really Care?"

After a while, his sobbing stopped. "You know, when the awfulest comes, you think about it for a while, then you think 'I gots my life to live now.' So you gets yourself up and goes about doing it. The weirdest thing is ... over there ... I'd not take as long a time to think that way. Here, at home with you, I was beginning to be human. I'm right proud of that, Little Bit. To know you bring out the best in me." He gave her a sad, sweet smile.

"I'm glad of that," Betsy said into his left ear. Into his right ear she whispered, "Know what the best thing is? I don'ts. I think I do and then you find something else to amaze me by. Crowds right over me."

Smythe laughed. "Crowds right over the both of us, Little Bit. Let's go crowding and see what we can come up with."

"You're on!" Betsy knew her face lit up like he wanted. "First, though, I thought Cinder was an angel. You just called her a bitch."

"Yeah, well, that's a compliment. Means she's hot for her man. We go back a ways, you know." Then Smythe hugged her and called her hot. "Like an angel," he said. As if she did not know.

tEDDY

Once, when he was younger, there had been a real bad time on the mountain. It ended in a bad way. Billy got hurt because of it. The reason he knew that was because he and Billy got to drinking in the back of Session's barn. Back in Crossing Place from where he was no longer at.

"What about my hometown?" Teddy stared hard into Tina's surprised face.

"It's here in the paper, Teddy. Sure looks like your old man."

Teddy grabbed the newspaper from Tina before it turned to stone. He looked first at the drawing. Then at the date. Then back at the drawing. After a while, he raised his face so Tina's eyes could see the hurt there. He could see she felt scared for him.

"I'm sorry, Teddy. Stirring you up like that. Forget what I said. Let's go out. Just go do something. OK, Teddy?" Her words sounded tentative. Unsure.

He'd told her of his old feelings. The ones that brought anger and wanting to lash out at something, anything, to take away what was still mixed up inside him. Once he would have yelled at people that were close to him. Gotten them so mad at him that they would go away and leave him alone. Back then, he would have felt like picking Tina up and throwing her away. But he felt different, now. Besides it wasn't about his old man. Or about him. This time it was about Marley. What was it, a year or more, since he left town?

"Crossing Place. Funny thing. Right in this paper. Just when I thought I'd put that all behind me. There's that old bastard. Just look at him. It's like he got the wind knocked out of his sails. Marley. My little sister. Half sister. She either run off like I did or got lost on the mountain. I get the shit kicked out of me and she gets a ride in an airplane." Teddy threw back his head and laughed. Laughed at the idea of a little twit like Marley making that man cry. Laughed because for the first time in years he felt compassion for his family.

Tina seemed frozen in her perch upon their tattered old couch

151

"Hey," he said in his smooth voice. "It's OK. If you want, we can go out. Sometime, though, I gotta make a call. Call my Momma. Find out about Marley. Talk."

"Is it OK if I ask you who else you recognize in this drawing?"

And so he did. Billy Trent. "I'll be damned. You're one smart lady, Tina. Mind if we stay in and enjoy each other's company this fine evening? I don't have to bother Momma. I can call Billy. What a girl you are. Hand me a problem, then solve it yourself. Man, oh, man, am I a lucky man."

"I'll say," teased Tina. "You're so lucky. Why go out for steak, when we got leftovers."

"Oh, man! We're both lucky."

fRIEDA

Her mother came with unexpected news. On being married again!

"I'm bringing Yung over for Christmas dinner so you and Dean and Kade can meet him. Oh, also Kevin. I must warn you. He's Asian, a scholar, and an artist. He's never been married, but has had a great many affairs. Of which there is to be no discussion. He's looking forward to being a grandfather, but I convinced him he had to find out if it was OK with the twins. You never know. Now, Frieda, you know how hard it is to stay on a diet at Christmas. Could we not have pecan pie this year?"

"For Heaven's sake, Mom. I never liked pecan pie. You have my vote," laughed Frieda.

"Good. Yung's a vegetarian. How about if we have shrimp on the menu?"

"Shrimp? OK."

"Nothing alcoholic?"

"Oh, no. Not even mouth wash."

"Frieda. Are you alright with this? We may be getting married in Vegas on New Years. Try this on for me. Mrs. Victoria Abbott Harrington Coumbs to marry Yung Li. I've never been in Vegas. I'd like to see Wayne Newton sing Danke Schoen."

Frieda reached across her kitchen table to hold her mother's hand. "It's a great agenda. I hope Yung can keep up with you."

"Don't be silly, Frieda. I'm one step behind him." Victoria winked at her daughter. "It's an Asian joke, my dear. However, Yung takes it seriously. He's in a wheelchair."

On the very same day, along comes Amy with her story.

"Oh, Frieda, I need such a favor, you will laugh away a month of Sundays. You know that jogging suit? The maroon one? The one you got at the swap? It's real heavy and would be just the thing for Clyde's big old eighteen wheeler. Could you spare it?"

"I'm not laughing, Amy. I'm dumbstruck. Who's Clyde?"

"You know him. Comes by Murphy's? Drives a truck? Well, he's one of those Marley rescuers. He rode off with Shute."

"Oh. Yes. He caught Dannel Harris! I don't think he'd fit into my jogging suit, Amy. Why, he's bigger than Vern!"

"He is; but Dannel waylaid Shawn. The suit's for me. I'm going on a long haul with Clyde ... who helped at the tent. All the way to Vegas. Are you laughing now?"

"No. No, I'm crying. Crying inside. Because I'm ... I'm .... Oh, shucks!" Frieda gave Amy a hug. Then they hugged again.

"Thanks, Frieda. I needed that. Now, go fetch that suit!"

Later that afternoon Ellen came home from school, saying she had two stories. She said, "Marley has had a phone call from Teddy."

"Oh, dear. I hope it didn't upset her. I never thought they got along."

"Of course not," sighed Ellen. "Unfortunately not all siblings get along like Sam and I. Marley was happy to hear from him, Mrs. Young. It seems they both did a lot of growing this past year. Well, months for Marley. And she said he called after he saw my drawing about her in the newspaper. All the way to New York!"

"New York? Well that's fine, just fine, Ellen. I'm glad for both of you. For the three of you."

"Now see here, Mrs. Young. I got over my crush on Teddy way before he run off. Don't you be bringing that up to Momma. I think she has a residue tanked up over that. I don't want to even think about that no more."

"Bring what up?"

"Oh, I had a crush on him is all. He didn't deserve it. He never showed me the slightest interest. I put his picture on my wall and Momma about tore it down. The wall. She tore that picture off so hard. Now he sees my cartoon in New York. Funny how things go, isn't it? Know what? I got a special letter from someone from New York. Charissa Bisset. She sent me an application for a scholarship to her University. She's an art teacher there. She wants to recommend my going there. What do you think of that? She's a friend of Ms Smythe."

"I think it's wonderful, Ellen. Goodness, you went by that wall thing so fast, I hardly had a chance to laugh. It sounded so funny to me."

"Oh, oh." Ellen gave Frieda a hug. "Another suggestion for an art thing. You're right. I'm on it. And...and...maybe Mr. Young can tell you the other story. It's ... a harder one."

Ellen's expression seemed as animated as her cartoons. Not lost on Frieda was the other look, with a sad frown, that slipped out as she darted away.

When Kevin told her about Cinder Smythe, Frieda felt the clock had stopped ticking. Yes, the war. She had not kept track of it. Now it had hit close to home. For this, Cinder needed more than chicken soup. Kevin said Cinder was not alone. Later, Frieda sobbed alone for her.

Then Billy came over for dinner and talked to Kevin about a call from Teddy. Frieda just listened. "I never thought he'd up and leave town," sighed Billy. "But you must know it must've done him good. He's got a girl, a maintenance job with good pay, and made up with Marley. Caught her with her guard down, I reckon. Sometimes that's the best way, eh, Ruby?" He seemed to be waiting for Ruby to jump in and say something.

Ruby folded her arms across her apron. "Ellen got an application to attend a college in New York. She also got an invitation to come for an interview and a campus visit. January. All because of Marley. And her cartoons. I'm hoping we can go together. That is, if Sammy will be OK here and if you can find someone to help out while we're gone. Someone who can cook and make beds. Billy said he'd pay for our trip."

Frieda burst into laughter. "I'm sorry," she confessed. "This is the third trip I've heard tell of today. Two trips to Vegas. Amy with Clyde. Grandmumma with an extraordinary man to be Grandpa Yung to Kade and Dean. Now you all to New York. I say, whatever it takes. Go. Things will work out around here. We are a lucky family. But, you know, we need to get you some prime rib clothing. Do we have time for a clothing swap?"

Then Ruby and Ellen were laughing. Kade and Dean laughed. Billy and Kevin laughed with Dean and Kade, too, without knowing why. Frieda could not stop laughing, yet she knew why. Things were getting too complicated to take lying down. Life got to her big time!

When it comes, it comes right at you.
This is the way of life.
Going along.
Taking stock.
Then poof
It's more than looking both ways
before crossing the street
It's remembering to laugh. To take stock.
To share. Be there for yourself and others.
This is the way of life.
When it comes, it comes right at you.

sMYTHE

"Hold on, Emily," said Smythe. "I don't want to give my angel any false hope. I don't know what's more wrong than your best friend being dead. Except, maybe he ain't."

"How do you mean that?" Emily said she, like him, didn't want to stir Cinder up with false hope.

"Look. Between you and me, there are miracles when it comes to war. And there are screw ups. I was thinking about the dates. I know where Rudd was when I left. We were not in camp, you see. I don't know when he was heading back. It was pretty tense where we were. So, see if the dates match up. If they seem...well, just call me back. I gots to know. We'll go from there."

"It doesn't seem fair," said Betsy. "But at least you ain't gots those guns all around you whilst you're trying to save your man."

"Can you get me another cup of that fine coffee whilst I wait for Emily's call?"

"Correction. Whilst we wait. I knows. I see you and I knows."

There was no need for Smythe to do more than let a smile draw her close.

Smythe listened carefully to Emily's business like voice as she gave him the dates. "His letter says the 11th. You were here on the 16th. That was five days difference. The Death Notice is dated on the 18th."

"Does it say when?" Smythe meant...but could not say...when he died.

"The signed letter with it says more on that. It tells about a blast on base camp. It says not all causalities were identified. It says that...that Rudd was among the missing."

"And it says he died for his country. Thank you very much," finished Smythe.

"Yes."

"So, he did make it back to camp. It was only a slim one he didn't. I'll be returning on the 4th. Tell my angel, I'll be waiting on her column. Thank you, Emily."

Smythe had to hold back what he really felt; so he sipped his coffee. He thought he had done well in spite of losing his best friend.

eMILY

"Thank you, Smythe," said Emily. Cinder was at her elbow when she put down the phone.

"Was that Smythe? What'd he want?"

"He wanted you to know he was going back on the 4th. He said to tell his angel he'd be waiting for her column. He actually said, 'I'll be waiting on her column'."

An inaudible sigh sunk with Cinder into a kitchen chair. "I hope so. I am, too."

"You sure you don't want something, Cinder? I can give you something." Emily knew the answer.

"No. I think Smythe is right. I'll just sit by my window and write my column."

"He might be right about something else, Cinder. I mean, about Rudd. The timing of when he was not in camp. Yet, he thinks Rudd probably did have time to get back there before it got hit. Smythe's going back on the fourth. He says it's only a slim chance and maybe I should not have told you. Miracles do not come often in war he said."

"In a little while I'm going to make some Alfredo sauce to go with those left over noodles. I was thinking, Emily, since we're grounded for Christmas, Racine and I, we should rent some old movies, eat our way through the holidays. And when you come back, we can enjoy hearing how your sister's family enjoyed all those presents you got them."

"Presents!" Emily whisked herself away to wrap those presents. She was leaving for Connecticut in the morning. Suddenly, her spirits were back on track. She did not feel guilty about being happy. Cinder had made it her goal.

jOSH

Since Marley's fall on the mountain, Josh had made it a point to know the people in his town. Find out their innards. He had volunteered to clear tables at Murphy's during the holidays just so's he could get up close and personal to people without anyone's knowing. Then Rachel asked him if he'd like a paying job at the greenhouse. Josh, just barely off drugs and fearful of backsliding, felt proud to be trusted to watch the fires at the greenhouse. Amy left a carefully worded list. Check the pipes.

Monitor the plants. The routine could have been easy; but the temperature dropped below zero. With the wind chill, it was relentlessly cold. Josh was relentless, too. He got Billy to come in with him one time, just to be sure he was doing things right. It was Billy who was always there to help him put perspective on things. He wanted to talk to Billy about Amy. In a small town like Crossing Place, news travels fast. Folks on Amy's answering machine were just bursting to be first in telling her something. "Could be true. But gossip, really," Josh quietly confided to Billy as they sat by the boiler to eat the lunch Ruby had packed for them.

"Yep. That's a failing of most folks, I reckon. Needing a sounding board for being just a whisker away from knowing something. Or need a place to park it. Can hurt sometimes. Can help sometimes. Amy usually knows the difference. When things got all tangled up over my accident on the mountain, it was Amy who set things straight. She got a fine reputation for sticking up for me and got me a chance to heal in peace."

"Yeah?" By now Josh had heard about twenty versions of what had happened to Billy on the mountain. "Did Fly learn anything from it?"

"Well, Fly's on track now. He's been there, done that. Best law officer in the County. I kid you not. He and Amy run this town. There's still friction between them; but I know they would stand by each other if push comes to shove. Helps me sleep at night."

"Yeah? It's fascinating. How people are. Like unreduced fractions. Or wholes hard to find because the parts don't always add up."

"What you doing? Comparing people with fractions? You know, Ellen's putting up a portfolio of her cartoons. Taking them with her to New York. I'm wondering how she would feel about that fraction idea."

"So's you know, Billy. I already have her take on that. She and I talk about it from time to time. Sammy, too. Just in case."

"I understand. You don't want any rumors to get back to Marley."

"Whoa, Billy. I and Marley: drug users. All done now because what happened to her scared it out of both of us. Besides, she and Dannel are pals again. And I'm right proud of him to stand up for her as he has done. She's sure turned out well. Not even a fake leg will keep her from being the most beautiful girl in town. She'll never be a faded rose. I need Sammy ... see, he might .... " Josh faltered. Felt his face flush.

"You mean, intentions? Sammy is too slow to think that way."

Josh took a deep breath. He might as well trust Billy. Ellen sure did. "I mean, Sammy is a camera bug. He's good at it. I'm saving up to get him a video camera. That's why Amy asked me to watch this place."

"Whoa. I didn't know that about Sammy. Interesting."

"Here's the plan, Billy. If I can get a scholarship to go to Tech school. In Presque Isle? Studying Media? Sammy will be in Crossing Place. Taking pictures. Ellen will be in New York. Studying Art. It will all come together someday. We're doing a documentary. The three of us. Sum of the Parts: A History in Crossing Place. I got the idea from you."

"Go for it," said Billy, although his smile came with a shrug of his shoulders.

"Thanks, Billy. There's something else I gotta tell you. We both owe it to Amy to keep it a secret. You and me."

"She in on this, too?"

"No. But she's a great role model." Josh walked Billy over to Amy's bulletin board. Newspaper clippings were arranged neatly on one side. **The Country Chatoyant***(Shaw-toy-awnt)* columns. From one of them Josh read: ***But none can walk in your shoes as you must do.***

"See, Billy. It's autographed. Special to Amy Shirley. Cinder Lorraine Smythe. Ms Smythe! She writes a newspaper column! Imagine that?"

"Whew," said Billy. "All this talent right here amongst us. What's this town coming to?"

"Exactly," said Josh with a big smile on his face. "Mind if I quote you on that?"

kEVIN

"I have something I have to tell you Kevin."

"Oh, Geeze, Frieda." His throat suddenly became dry. And he was afraid to listen. Afraid not to. Frieda's smile softened the way he looked at her. A warm glow rested upon her cheeks. Above her pink top.

"My intent was to surprise you, Kevin. Not now, but later. I am in need of your help now."

"I always like to be the go-to-guy, My Dear. Whatever it is, sit here on my couch and we will have a go at it." He turned off the TV.

Frieda laughed then and did as he bid her. Between them she put a white package. It looked like a book. She told him it was her book.

"Not for me?"

"I wrote it."

"You wrote a book? Is it a poetry book?"

"Yes ... a book of poems ... usually soft and quiet thoughts. Poems about growing. For our twins. About parenting twins. And how they see their world."

"I like this surprise, Frieda. Need help in finding a publisher?"

"Oh, it's already set, you see. But there is this one poem, Kevin, that I'm concerned about ... because ... because it comes in from outside of my quiet little nest. The thoughts were quite powerful, but jumbled. From you, of Marla. Then when Cinder lost her Rudd. I had to write this. I need your input."

Kevin took a deep breath. "But, my drinking was bothering you and then there was this pink sweater thing! We are stronger now, remember? 'Team Frieda!' Let me read the poem. Is it a rainbow?"

"Oh!" Frieda's already flushed face, flushed more. She laughed. Threw her arms around Kevin. Like to strangle him with her hug. She told him she wanted to surprise him. From being the keeper of the list of things to do and become a writer. Many emotions coming between them. "But you surprised me! That's it! A rainbow. Be right back."

True to her word, she returned right away. Kevin read what she had written .... twice. Frieda sat with her hands folded in her lap.

"One word, Freida, phenomenal. You. You are the rainbow and if you don't mind, I must tell you, it is no secret what you can do!"

"Oh, Kevin, did you make that up?"

"Nope. I need some practice, but I can learn."

Kade and Dean bounced in from their snowball fight with Ellen.

"Who won?" asked Frieda.

"You know who won, Mumma," said Kade.

"Ellen," said Dean.

"They always say that," said Ellen. "So's they get a rematch."

"Well, how about some chicken soup?" Asked Frieda.

Kevin thought and then said, "Phenomenal."

"Pen.norm.un.al," tried Dean.

"Phone.in.meal," tried Kade.

"Phen.om.en.al," said Ellen. "I win!"

fRIEDA

Team Frieda was alive and well! Published writer. No secret! Her mother had her outfit ready for Frieda's first book presentation! Coming soon at her college campus. The poem she had shared with Kevin.was added, especially, as she requested 'for an older side to my twins'.

> *Outside*   *of*
> *where I am,*   *an*
> *unknown harm is wasting away a country.*

> *Life,*
> *dribbled and dibbled in the pocket.*
> *Changed, forever.*

> *This I know:*
> *"The unknown*   *will*
> *be met in a better light*   *when*
> *there is someone with whom to filter it."*

> *And this I have seen:*

"Sometimes we think people
are as fragile as soap bubbles;
until we see the rainbows inside of them."

!What happens, then in February, gots to do with snow angels!

~10~

cINDER

"Ho! Ho! Ho!" quoth the mailman when he came upon them playing in the snow.

"Ho, yourself," called Racine, shaking the snow from her coat and leggings. "Come on in and make your mark. There's room for more. Vern and Rachel will be flying over soon. We want them to see our snow angels. As many as we can get."

It was an unusual request. Dozens of snow covered kids, from the apartment building and nearby, yelled gleefully at him to make one.

"Alright. This doesn't mean I have to hand out Valentine cards afterwards?"

The kids all laughed. One of them took his picture as he plopped down in the snow with his mail bag on his stomach and spread his arms and feet to make an angel shape. Everyone laughed again because he couldn't get up. A camera popped when Cinder and Racine dusted him off; another when they sent him on his way.

"He's nice of him," said Racine happily, when the favorite mailman of the day was out of sight.

"If you think he's nice in snow, you should see him in shorts," whispered Cinder in Racine's ear. From the twinkle in Racine's eye, it was clear she had thought of that.

Then, the plane flew over. Vern and Rachel saw them, for the plane came around again. The kids were so excited, they threw snow in the air and cheered.

Afterwards, hot chocolate and donuts came for all from Murphy's.

Afterwards, those that could stayed to watch the Harry Potter movie Cinder and Racine had rented for their February vacation stay-at-home. Afterwards, Emily came in with crumpled mail Cinder had left beside her door. Racine and Cinder watched the movie again with Emily.

Afterwards, Cinder had a dream of the man who saved her. Only this time he kissed her. And she smelled relish. And his laugh was abrupt and burstingly contagious. Cinder awoke with an urge to sort through some things she had kept in a box under her desk. Things with memories of Rudd. On top was a favorite book. *Wildflowers of New England*. Chester A. Reed, 1912. Colors of the Brown-eyed Susan adorning the brown leather cover were still true. Rudd had given this small bound book to her when he gave her an invitation to move in with him. She kept his note in this book. He had written:

> " 'The great thing in this world is not so much where we are, but in what direction we are going.' Quoting Oliver Wendell Holmes. So why not move in with me? Really, why not?"

Anothr letter in her box. gave her power of attorney in case a bundle came from Iraq. She reached under it and pulled out Rudd's favorite woolen shirt. Dark green. He liked the way it set off her red hair. Here, also, was her copy of the *Desiderata*. Cinder's heart filled with she and Rudd's making snow angels in February as she closed the box. The wire ring, Rudd had made for her, felt warm upon her finger.

She spoke softly, then. "I came here to Crossing Place so I could be near the mountain. I like it here, Rudd. I have a niche here. They got chicken soup, too. There's always something going on. I can e-mail my friends and they can e-mail me. It's a good place for me to be. So this is where I'll be.

Looking for the rest of the story. I love you, Rudd Wallace Vachon. Right here." Touching the ring to her heart, she drew in a body lifting breath.

This then was to where Cinder was as she sat before her window to finish the piece she had started before Christmas. For Rachel and Vern Paselli. For Emily, Racine, and always Amy. For the wonder of Josh and Dannel and Ellen and for understanding Marley. For Mrs. Kingsbury, who subbed for her and confessed she knew Cinder's secret. For Billy and his bedroom eyes. For all the wonderous people in Crossing Place and her dear friends, Charissa and Carla, at the other corners of the triangle. For her soul-cousin Smythe and his Little Bit. For snow angels. And always for Rudd. As the *Country Chatoyant.*

> *In my heart there is a place where sweetness lies, hope rules, and goodwill wins. Yesterday's sweetness hugged me. Goodwill lifted me up. Then suddenly hope became so small, its presence eluded me. For I was sadly shaken. Today I see fresh tracks in the snow upon the walk. Should snow cover those tracks there will come others. It pleases me to know that. This little thing in life that gives me hope. It's like opening an unwrapped present. From my heart to your heart, I can go on. Thank you. I can rest assured in that.*

Cinder felt pride for pulling the simple, human trait of hope from her heart for others like her who waited. News of late flashed images of war prisoners, clad in orange jump suits, chained, hooded, stored in a cemented, barbed wire enclosure. A strange, stagnant place. Quantanamo Bay? Abu Ghraib? Somewhere on the Eastern tip of Cuba. She thought of the movie, *They Shoot Horses, Don't They?*

Then Cinder looked through the crumpled mail Emily had left on her counter. Shopping circulars, some bills and a crisp blue envelope with a stamp showing a plane that seemed to be rippling over the snow white earth and leaving angel wings in its wake. It made her smile as she slipped her forefinger under the seal to release the contents.

And then she was banging on Emily's door, shouting for all the world to hear! "Emily! Wake up! You won't believe...Emily! A miracle! Smythe! Oh, my God, Emily! Wake up!"

....and it took more than waiting.

Read Emily, able to cry openly over the *Chatoyant* column amongst co-workers. One of them offered her his handkerchief. Then they had some coffee. Then a marvelous thing happened. She and Jepher exchanged phone numbers.

It took a miracle! I need to remember this then. This aura. Helpless, hurtful, hopeful little thing. Eclipsed by the bigger world of war. Being exactly it, though. More to feel, give and hope for in this space, in this time. Knowing, always, we do not wait alone.

"Awesome!" Josh clipped this *Chatoyant* column. As did Amy for her Niomi. As did Ellen, Marla and Charissa. For different notions. As to why Rachel made sure there were extra newspapers at Murphy's when *Chatoyant* columns were published. For when customer's wanted a copy of the *Chatoyant* words. Words that were always fostering strong feelings. Many of them affirmed when each read on.

Once you've climbed upon that Wall of Peace, you've laid your claim for a miracle, no matter how long it takes you to see...what form it takes...you can go on.

Billy said the column could have been written of Ruby and Frieda. "You both have miracles in your families. Always room for more."

Ruby smiled at Billy over her coffee cup.

Out Frieda's window they could see Kade and Dean. See Dean and Kade. Building a snow house with their father. Her Kevin, who cared enough. Enough to last a life ... a life time.

My Husband,
making it a priority to be there for his family.
So. too, shall I.

"You want me to what?" Then Rachel lay beside him in the snow. Joining him out of the box. To make snow angels.

Carla lit candles by her porch windows. Waved to her neighbors. Especially one of them.

Beyond a window, behind her desk, Samantha saw him coming. A smile lighted her round, sweet face. How long had she known, Fly ... Bob Fly ... Sheriff Bob Fly ...wondered.

Shute smiled at a lady whose perfect geode necklace cast lights across his balding head. He made plans to ask Pearl soon. Very soon.

At Crocker's, cars were parked in the driveway and under the street lights on Dawson Street. Not an unusual sight at Crocker's. But this was a special gathering. For Marla's party. For her home coming!

A beautiful little miss, sans makeup, re-read the letter she had copied to send to Cinder. From her man, Smythe. News about Rudd. Filled with much pride and pain. She could not bring herself to phone Cinder. Warn her of the blue envelope's coming. She knew Smythe's Angel would understand. Understand how holding a letter would be better than the telling of it. She had seen. She knew. She knew Cinder's faith in the Wall of Peace included closure. As did her own.

Somewhere, over the water, amongst heavy breathing, staring faces and smothered voices, spoke this man, this soldier, standing without crutches and holding onto the arm of a wounded soldier ... swathed in bandages about his face and upper body, beside him upon a stretcher ... steadying himself. "I wants you to know folks, I know's something about Miracles. This here white man? He's gonna be my cousin. Ain't it a miracle?" Tired, worried eyes looked. Waited in static silence. Then came that laughter, abrupt and burstingly contagious!

I quote thee of fine will and testament,   *"My amulet is in my heart. And it is you."*

      Cinder lay under her coverlets, anchored. Her eyes shut against the morning light. Waiting to feel him beside her. Home. She dreamed of taking small steps as he had asked of her. Could she be dreaming?

      She could cuddle down deep under her coverlets, where she could laugh and cry as well and as long as one could do when alone in a little bed where none could shush her or cuddle her or worry that she needed chicken soup!

      Here, it was safe to dream of Betsy and Smythe. Of their wearing white and waving at her from a small plane flying high above the mountain. They looked like angels. Indeed the shadow from the plane as it flew closer seemed to be rippling over the snow white earth and leaving angel wings in its wake. There was Emily, standing in the doorway with her red bathrobe over her shoulders and the arms of it pulled to her waist, telling Cinder, "Yes! That's what people in Crossing Place do in February ... make snow angels."

      What Emily did not say was the mostest perfect reaction Cinder could have hugged her for! Together, they called Carla and Charissa who suddenly became teenagers again! Saying things like, "Wow!" And, "Wow!" And Racine? Racine said she was speechless but would make up for that soon enough. All of them agreed there could never be any finer words than what her cousin, Smythe ... as true a soul as any of Cinder's friends on the Triangle knew ... had written in his letter to Betsy:

"Know this, Little Bit,
Us Smythe's stick together!
That's what we do for our cousins.".

When she looked up, she saw her father, home
with her family. When she grew up,
she thought of a plane, flying over the
mountains to bring her soldier home.
Then she created a town to tell about this.
From Joan Philbrick Goodwin

This on NANCY, the Author, from Terry Philbrick Smith

Back in the fifties, attending our two room school in Knox, I remember when Mr. Harris turned Friday afternoons into a Literature party. Everyone, from grade four to eight, had to share something. Mom always helped me, or I never could have done it. Joan and Nancy, my big and little sisters, loved it. Once, Joan wrote a scary poem and performed it in her black costume and huge mask like she was the Witch from Lost Halloweens. Kids laughed and screamed and hid under their desks! Nancy's first offering was a funny story about Cowboys and Indians. She even had sound effects. Everyone clapped, especially the boys because they hated this day as much as I did. But I like remembering what happened after school. We came in from our chores and saw what Mom had written under the A+ on Nancy's paper. "Who wrote this? Fix your spelling." Nancy did, with Joan's help. I couldn't believe it. So I asked why. Mom said, "If it is worth writing, it is worth writing well." Joan said that Nancy had a long way to go, but she would get there someday. Mom looked at me and said, "Just like those bedtime stories you tell the kids, Terry. When you or Joan fall asleep, I can hear Nancy finishing them." I guess Nancy, the author, stayed awake and got there ... with tHIS!

www.ingramcontent.com/pod-product-compliance
Lightning Source LLC
Chambersburg PA
CBHW020424290526
45785CB00002B/710